Cambridge Elements

Elements in Ancient East Asia
PEOPLE: Family, Gender, Class, and the Individual

ARCHAEOLOGICAL STUDIES ON GENDER IN EARLY EAST ASIA

Mandy Jui-man Wu
Hanover College
Katheryn M. Linduff
University of Pittsburgh

Shaftesbury Road, Cambridge CB2 8EA, United Kingdom

One Liberty Plaza, 20th Floor, New York, NY 10006, USA

477 Williamstown Road, Port Melbourne, VIC 3207, Australia

314–321, 3rd Floor, Plot 3, Splendor Forum, Jasola District Centre, New Delhi – 110025, India

103 Penang Road, #05–06/07, Visioncrest Commercial, Singapore 238467

Cambridge University Press is part of Cambridge University Press & Assessment, a department of the University of Cambridge.

We share the University's mission to contribute to society through the pursuit of education, learning and research at the highest international levels of excellence.

www.cambridge.org
Information on this title: www.cambridge.org/9781009533546

DOI: 10.1017/9781108987486

When citing this work, please include a reference to the DOI 10.1017/9781108987486

First published 2024

A catalogue record for this publication is available from the British Library

ISBN 978-1-009-53354-6 Hardback
ISBN 978-1-108-98739-4 Paperback
ISSN 2632-7325 (online)
ISSN 2632-7317 (print)

Archaeological Studies on Gender in Early East Asia

Elements in Ancient East Asia

DOI: 10.1017/9781108987486
First published online: December 2024

Mandy Jui-man Wu
Hanover College

Katheryn M. Linduff
University of Pittsburgh

Author for correspondence: Mandy Jui-man Wu, wuju@hanover.edu

Abstract: Gendered archaeology in Asia has been studied by archaeologists since the 1990s and scholars have posed questions such as the role and construction of gendered identities in ancient societies. In this Element, the authors review secondary literature, report on to what stage the research has evolved, evaluate methodologies, and use the concept of networking to examine the issues across East Asia, including China, Mongolia, Korea, Japan, and Taiwan. Interestingly, those literatures are not entirely parallel with each other – the authors found, for example, that archaeological investigation was largely bound by national guidelines, by local intellectual traditions, and by changing historiographic interpretations of past events, as well as funding. The complexion of recent studies on gender and archaeology in Asia has often been focused on providing a framework for a grand narrative of each national "civilization" as the emergence of institutional political structures, including traditional values placed on men and women.

Keywords: gender, ancient Asia, archaeology, women, identity

ISBNs: 9781009533546 (HB), 9781108987394 (PB), 9781108987486 (OC)
ISSNs: 2632-7325 (online), 2632-7317 (print)

Contents

1 Introduction

1.1 Overview

The roles of men and women in our societies are observable in everyday life to all of us, but the construction of attitudes toward "proper" behavior for genders is culture-based and has a history that is often elusive, as it is often not recorded directly. Gender constructions are the result of and affected by political, economic, ideological, and religious thinking, the law, urban and rural life, social structure, leisure and entertainment, family life, birth, marriage, death and burial, health, nutrition and food, education, and many other aspects of our lives. These are not always readily observable in the past lives of those unearthed through archaeological investigation.[1] As was proposed in 1984 by Margaret Conkey and Janet Spector, archaeology can substantiate sets of culture-specific beliefs about the meaning of masculine and feminine, about the capabilities of men and women, about their power relations, and about their appropriate roles in society (Conkey and Spector 1984: 1). We ask if this idea has guided archaeological research on gender in East Asia.

In preparing this Element, we examined historical and current intellectual concepts that have guided researchers who study gender in archaeology in ancient East Asia. Immediately, we recognized that the characters for sex and gender are the same in Chinese, Japanese, and Korean (性別),[2] such that distinctions between discerning sex and gendered behavior have not always been sought. Interestingly, the words in Mongolian (and Russian) do mark that difference (sex = секс, gender = хүйс; and in Russian, sex = секс, gender = пол, род) and may be tied to a more complex understanding of social order in literature in these languages (see Section 2.4 on Mongolia). Even though looking for patterns in the expression of gender and learning how that might be preserved in archaeological settings might have been our initial goal, we found that such a focus has not directed most studies to date in East Asia. Discovering and recording distinctive patterns that marked sexes in past burial practice has dominated the research, and that is an important first step, but further advances in the study of gender will require clearer conceptualizations of gender as a socially constructed facet of societies and individuals. An understanding of gender as intrinsically tied to conceptions of fluid and multiple

[1] The most recent comprehensive, synthetic historical study of everyday life in East Asia is focused on China in the Han dynasty and outlines many of these issues (Poo 2018). Poo Mu-chou's volume includes a section on gender relations (Poo 2018: 186–206).

[2] We have inserted Asian orthography in the text and Bibliography for all transliterated words, papers and book titles, proper names of authors, sites names, and so on, according to the local writing system.

identities, whether national, political, personal, ethnic, cultural, or otherwise, could lead to contextualizing gendered behavior further historically.

Although we searched for and hopefully have found most of what has been published about gender in archaeology across East Asia, we have not found, or do not know how to locate, everything. For instance, following 2004 when the first full set of edited articles on gender in early China appeared in English and then in Chinese (Linduff and Sun 2004, 2006), we documented almost 200 articles published in Chinese. By contrast, we found thirty or fewer articles focused on gender in each of the other countries, whether in local or other languages. In this Element, we concentrate on local language publications while illustrating both the methods and the proposed results with case studies and noting the impact of thinking from outside the region where relevant.[3]

We report patterns of interest and analysis in scholarship and group research by what we think is the foundational infrastructure of that research and analysis. Even though East Asia was historically and is currently a region comprised of culturally, ethnically, politically, and socially complex societies where gender as studied by archaeologists might lead to quite varied conceptions of social behavior, we found that such understanding has been unevenly initiated across the region. Historical texts, whether contemporary with the early societies on which they supposedly report or not, hold an especially privileged place both in the definition of topics for research and in the interpretation of archaeological data. Those historical texts most often report a uniform view of "proper behavior" for all men and women within a homogenizing notion of the target culture. In addition, archaeological methods vary for the collection of data and most often the focus is not an effort to examine issues of gender. Some scholars make use of ethnographic parallels in their analyses, but these are rarely accompanied by discussions of anthropological theory. Perhaps the most compelling recent change in research methods is the application of newer scientific testing that has led to an understanding of the movement of peoples, family lineages, food, diet, and health disparities across a population, including class, ethnicity, and genders. Those test results are often added to other older styles of historical-culture analyses related to gender. For instance, cranial morphologies and/or typologies are often used to build interpretations of "ethnicity" and "gender" even though other more certain testing methods that determine sex have neither initially nor

[3] Although we have concentrated our searches on those published in local languages and/or local scholars, we also mention publications in other languages that we found have been especially persuasive in the study of gender and archaeology in East Asia regardless of national affiliation. We also note the comprehensive bibliographies compiled by Robin Yates and Danni Cai (2018), although these are focused on publications on women and gender in China and written in Western languages only, and do not focus on archaeological studies.

consistently been applied.[4] Assertions about femininity and masculinity have also sometimes been based on contemporary assumptions about gender roles. One such example is the telling of changes in the social order within the Marxist paradigm from matriarchy to patriarchy in late prehistory as applied in the People's Republic of China (PRC) since its establishment. Without archaeological data to confirm female leadership, gendered roles in households, or political positions in prehistoric China, explanations have been recognized as politically motivated to show the emergence of societal inequality and to bolster the necessity for the new socialist order (Shelach 2004).

As we were invited to review "women and gender in early East Asia," we had to determine what areas and periods we thought should be included and how we might best represent coherent ancient culture regions within them. We have chosen to look at the prehistoric era up to established state-level period societies, in part because these stages have received the most attention in archaeology and gender studies. We define the region in geographic and ethnocultural terms. Geographically, although culturally not entirely distinct from adjacent regions, East Asia consists of the eastern region of the Eurasian landmass and includes the modern states of China, Japan, Mongolia, North Korea, South Korea, and Taiwan. Often throughout history, the area lay within the Chinese sphere of influence and adopted the Chinese written script and calendar, although each modern nation-state included has aimed to establish its own identity. Significantly, in addition, East Asia borders geographically on Siberia and the Russian Far East to the north, Southeast Asia to the south, South Asia to the southwest, and central Eurasia to the west. To the east is the Pacific Ocean and to the southeast is Micronesia (the Pacific Ocean island group classified as part of Oceania). Over time, mountains, prairies, formidable deserts, mighty river systems and seas, and climate changes have often formed political, cultural, as well as physical barriers to and within the region. Not surprisingly, complex ethnocultural mixes of peoples and societies emerged in antiquity that crossed these geographic areas, and many transregional connections still exist today. We have included notice of such intersections throughout as they figure directly in the formation of societies in East Asia and sometimes importantly in the shaping of notions of gender, but we have not surveyed those areas independently here.

Historically, societies in East Asia have been defined around issues associated with the rise and establishment of state-level polities and their peripheries. Of course, those important historical processes did occur. But prehistoric and early historic culture zones do not easily follow modern geographic or ethno-political

[4] See Section 2.1.

definitions, since we know that borders were fluid and peoples interacted not only at the edges of large communities or polities but even within the communities themselves through marriage, trade, and other forms of exchange. We know, for instance, that human cultural, biological, and genomic hybridity was the norm across East Asia as opposed to homogeneity (Pechenkina and Oxenman 2013). Genetically and culturally close communities inhabited the same or neighboring territories, the spaces once occupied by bygone states or empires that were and are often still united by the institutions as well as the political, economic, ideological, and notional ties of the past. The extent to which those legacies continue to influence the life of research today was clear in our survey of the published materials on gender, especially in the review of literature on ethnocultural and gendered life in early Taiwan. Although we know that interactive patterns of behavior existed and binary descriptions cannot adequately reflect the shape of the communities, polities, families, or archaeological recovery, East Asian authors have adhered stridently to report within modern national bounds and ethnocultural units created to advance national narratives.

Related to this nation-based reporting of archaeology, scholarship across the region has been profoundly affected by modern history in East Asia. Having witnessed the breakdown and dissolution of monarchies in China and Japan, social and political revolutions in Russia and China, the demise of colonial holdings, the downfall of the USSR, and two world wars, no part of East Asia was left unchanged. The subject of gender emerged there as in other parts of the world especially after World War II as a focused topic of research in the 1960s and 1970s as part of local reevaluations of social order that led to intensifying civil rights awareness. Increasingly globalized communication and economies worldwide have opened avenues of rapid exchange like never before. Although the results of this history manifest differently area by area, all were affected in some way by these events. For example, contemporary sociopolitical settings have, in our view, deeply influenced the way archaeological data are being understood and interpreted, as has the impact of the history and growth of “feminism” and/or consciousness of gender. And as has recently been reported about PRC female archaeologists (Hein et al. 2023: 559–590), we have noted the role of a growing awareness of and debate around “feminist” movements in the twentieth century across East Asia as one impetus for the study of gender as a factor in archaeological research.

These reflections arose after reviewing the secondary literature from China, Korea, Japan, Taiwan, and Mongolia that make use of archaeological data to reconstruct and interpret gendered actions of the past. Interestingly, those literatures are not entirely parallel with each other, and we found, for example, that archaeological investigation was largely bound by national regulations, by local intellectual traditions, and by changing historiographic interpretations of past events, as well as selective funding for research. Such circumstances have neither easily nor sometimes at all allowed for the study of ancient cultures and societal organization across modern national borders, thus negating a full understanding of the structure of whole ancient societies. This is, perhaps, one of the greatest deterrents to the study of ancient communities in regions that cross current state or even sometimes provincial borders.

Of course, observations of modern archaeologists and historians depend on what has been excavated and reported. Their reconstructions are affected by intellectual traditions brought to the task from each interpreter's past. Interestingly, we found that we needed to separate historical facts (archaeological data) as documented in excavated materials from reports and efforts that aimed to reconstruct historical knowledge (interpretation). The desire to record vs. the desire to understand and investigate the past varies from report to report. Although the two are not exclusive, they often are not mingled. Our hope is that by reviewing the current state of thinking about gender across East Asia, we can inspire the construction of the consequential historical experience of gendered behavior through which facts can be understood. That might take the form of more synthetic thinking on the part of collaborative teams of holders of specific information ready to be examined through an historical lens or the development of projects that take aim at gendered behavior at the outset. Many scientific tools and much more data are available to the archaeologist today, such that this sort of research is possible. We hope that this Element provides a useful starting point for additional future work in this direction.

1.2 Models from the Past and Current Goals

1.2.1 National Archaeologies

Contributions to the study of gender in archaeological contexts have increased over the past couple of decades and are naturally part of an overall interest in focusing on topics that reflect broad cross sections of populations across the globe. It is not surprising that current sociopolitical issues affecting the world at large have impacted the direction of the study of gender. The nature of recent studies in East Asia has often been focused on providing a framework for a grand narrative of each national "civilization," and underlying archaeological inquiry everywhere today, for instance, is the tension between nationalist vs. universalizing efforts to approach and then to interpret the data, including discussions of gender. Fieldwork in Asia, thus, is often driven by questions about how to identify the East Asian prehistoric and historic territorial borders/ spheres of cultures that are located within "Chinese," "Korean," "Japanese,"

"Taiwanese," or "Mongolian" archaeological spheres with the goal of developing histories of each "core" civilization.

Even so, the expansion in the recovery of regional and local archaeological materials all over East Asia has aided in nurturing lively debates that compare ancient societies across the globe and the multifaceted makeup of cultural formation. Whatever the nature of one's interpretation of culture and its formation and change, the point or points where such questions can be tested have benefited in the past several decades by being identified archaeologically. Unilinear theories of culture development have weakened as more and more diverse materials have been unearthed and regional paradigms have been made current (e.g., Migishima et al. 2011; Ōta-shi Kyōiku Iinkai 2012). Even so, what, where, and who contributed to any societal formation are questions that strike deep into nationalistic, as well as ethnic, sentiments and most often have not included ideas about the role of gender in these formative periods and structures.

In addition, globalizing propensities across the modern world have hastened the desire for comparative studies but have, unintentionally, also encouraged a competitive nationalist focus. This concern has also nurtured "network" studies that explore connectivity. Often this emphasizes the notion of nation-state interconnectivity through trade and expansion. More recently, "local" studies have emerged as a sort of antidote to global analysis, arguing that much can be learned by looking at interaction within centers regardless of size and complexity. In addition, household archaeological investigations have narrowed the lens even further to provide the capacity to examine gender roles in even more focused locales and individual households.

But perhaps most notably, culture norms and traditional historical narratives are often in conflict with other ways of studying topics that have to do with pre- and early historic social orders, including issues of gender. For instance, the Chinese socialist paradigm looks at history through a series of increasingly restrictive roles for women, from matriarchy to patriarchy, and assumes that those norms were ubiquitous across history. As reviewed by Shelach-Lavi (2004), this allows little room for revision or adjustment to the telling of history, since the progression is already described in the socialist mode of thinking. This conflict has bedeviled the study of gender and all its various iterations in China. Elsewhere in Asia, views about gender identity and roles are age-old and are also embedded in early literature as well as contemporary life and continue to affect how gender is interpreted when telling history. These views are further noted in each regional section in this Element.

These are not the only issues that retard interest in gender. The strong hold of traditional culture norms (even in the present) surely plays a part in attitudes toward the study of gender all across Asia. Interpretation of the sex of burial occupants is a case in point. Very often an assemblage of weapons and signs of leadership has led to an assignment of male sex, or likewise inclusion of weaving or cooking utensils has automatically suggested that the deceased was female. Although the technology that can determine biological sex is available across Asia, it is not uniformly used, in part because investigators suppose the sex of the deceased based on assumptions about artifacts in the tomb and social roles followed historically and up through today.

Sometimes even when scientific skills are applied (accelerator mass spectrometry [AMS] dating, DNA and genome analysis, strontium and stable isotope analysis [Wang M. et al. 2021: 35], and others discussed in the sections that follow), the results are reported without placing that information within the relevant historical context or considering how it might be used to reimagine constructed gender roles. Synthetic historical thinking is missing from many reports and would, of course, sometimes be difficult to accomplish as it usually requires collaborative teams of researchers not always available in local settings.

Even if one is certain that the sex identification in burial remains is correct and tested, excavations are often biased toward tombs of the elite class. If that analysis is used to generalize about roles across all society, differences in such features as age, culture background, ritual, status, societal or familial role, and so on could be easily missed.

Another measure of how well gender has been integrated into the study of early societies in East Asia can be found in a cross section of introductory texts, mostly in English. Examples from China include Li Liu's 2004 text on the Chinese Neolithic, which does consider gender status and roles when discussing the emergence of societal complexity in China, but her other introductory book with Xingcan Chen (2012) on early prehistory does not single out such issues. Gideon Shelach-Lavi's (2015) text on late prehistory through the Han, in contrast, does incorporate discussions of changes in gender roles across time when addressing the emergence of societal complexity. Likewise, posing questions about gender is uneven in introductory texts focused on Japan (Mizoguchi 2013) and Korea (Nelson 1995, 2003).

1.2.2 Differing Field Methodologies

The ability to discuss issues related to gender in a particular archaeological context depends in part on the field methodologies used. When developing an archaeological field project, the choice of whether to adopt a problem-based vs. an object-based line of inquiry draws attention to different goals and can result in different sorts of data. For example, gender or cultural difference is often reported in relation to how it affected a central core polity, thus benefiting traditional centrist views and "big" ideologies over discerning regional and diverse cultural terrains. Assumptions about the use and identification of objects might also simply preclude any more nuanced analysis of gender identity in an analysis of a habitation site or funerary settings.

Moreover, salvage recovery and Cultural Resource Management (CRM) work have frequently dominated archaeological activity across Asia, and this necessity has most often excluded research designs that focused on the collection of information on gender (for Japan, see, e.g., Nakazawa 2010). But if archaeologists are open and free to choose a place for survey and excavation, other decisions about what field methodologies might be adopted can be applied. Independent vs. collaborative or cross-national cooperation as well as the study and quest for fancy objects and other signs of elites vs. examining roles and lives of all members of the population are also important factors that influence whether gendered analysis can take place. Other matters such as broadscale excavation vs. targeted excavation, regional survey aimed at reconstruction of political and social structure vs. survey aimed at identifying potential sites for excavation, and attention to habitation sites vs. tombs make a difference in what is collected and thus if and/or what kind of gendered behavior can be determined.

Of course, the backbone of any archaeological inquiry is what is mapped, unearthed, and recorded – but any such work is not a simple search and rescue mission, as research priorities, training, and standard practice will influence what data are collected and intensively targeted. The results in East Asian countries, for instance, are clearly affected by certain priorities within specific national traditions. For example, the PRC embassy in the United States regularly and proudly reports on the "Oscars" of archaeology each year, as determined by a panel of experts, and the winners often represent tombs of the leadership (mostly male) of society filled with objects that are notable for their exotic materials or style, and worthy of curiosity that could be used to stimulate tourist trade, and that amplify the centralizing narrative of traditional histories (Embassy 2022). This sort of emphasis on elite culture has documented the trajectory and makeup of the supposed "cores" of Chinese, Korean, Japanese, Xiongnu, and Mongol civilizations. The current geopolitical atmosphere, including economic struggles and contending trade agreements represented by aggravated displays of power by force among modern nations across Asia, has fueled as well as financed the pursuit of nationalist agendas and its counterpart, the telling of mononuclear institutional and most often male-centered cultural development.

1.2.3 The Role of Texts

The force of tradition weighs heavily all across modern intellectual communities that examine early societies in East Asia. Historically, training for archaeologists has insisted on a great deal of focus on received texts, sometimes even to the exclusion of consideration of the surrounding archaeological context. Such dependence on received texts in the telling of history has shaped analyses of archaeological investigation across the region (Kinney 2014, 2018 [on China]; Nelson 1991 [on Korea]; Greaves 2020 [on Mongolia]; Barnes 2006 [on Japan]; plus vast numbers of articles and books on textual records, especially from China and Japan). One of the consequences of this focus has been to discourage the investigation of culture areas as defined in archaeological contexts in favor of discussions aimed at verifying textual accounts.

The imposition of traditional gender-centered interpretations from early texts has thus colored modern reconstructions of gendered behavior and roles. In all areas of East Asia, historians have traditionally been mostly male (Hein et al. 2023), and it is that gaze that has predominated. Details of gendered life were not often reported except in the most general terms in traditional histories. But there are indicators of how people lived in many cases, recorded in both textual accounts and archaeological debris that could breathe life into the data. The embedded hopes and ideals of groups in the society can with caution provide a backdrop for a more ground-up view of gendered lives as recorded in archaeological investigations. Currently, the study of excavated texts has made available a body of evidence that can elucidate gendered roles, identities, and status, especially in the case of inscriptions on excavated ritual bronzes. Very careful and astute readings of those texts have reasonably eked out information on marital patterns and roles of men and women, including attitudes toward core values and political power (e.g., Khayutina 2014, 2017; Sun 2021: 63–99). In addition, others have used material culture and objects as primary evidence of sociopolitical relationships (Sun 2021; Allard et al. 2018; Wu 2017 [on China]; Perrin 2010; Nelson 2008 [on Korea]; Ikawa-Smith and Habu 2002 [on Japan]; Miller 2024 [on Mongolia], and many others).

1.2.4 The Advent of Scientific Testing

Throughout East Asia today all sorts of scientific testing and analyses of remains, both human and material, are available and are often connected to issues of gender, but integration of these data with historical thinking is not always attempted. Heightened aspirations to preserve something of the past while at the same time recognizing the great advantages offered by new methodologies and technological applications have led directly to challenges to create accepted historical "knowledge." Impressive new studies have, however, revealed differing diets among men and women, or between classes and societal roles apparently based on attitudes about appropriate functions for men and women, and confirmed that the movement of women into cross-cultural marriage arrangements served for political advantage (e.g., Argawal and Glencross 2011a, 2011b; Holliman 2011; Pechenkina and Oxenham 2013). Reexamination of manners of classification, seriation, and chronologies and including carbon and AMS dating are underway and have the possibility to document more accurately many actions and changes in behavior both political and social.

1.2.5 Synthetic Studies

Synthetic cross-Asia studies characterize a direction of research that is especially demanding, if rewarding – requiring mastery of multiple languages, vast knowledge, and careful reasoning that sorts and then reports on patterns of behavior. In English, the 2015 edition of *Archaeology of East Asia: The Rise of Civilization in China, Korea, and Japan* by Gina Barnes was a major accomplishment, and one that has set a course for teaching and analysis across cultural and national borders since its first edition in 1993. The lesson from her book is that one can study Asia across modern national borders to see cultural boundaries and formation when guided by central anthropological questions about human behavior or bases of power manifest in political organization and social order. Likewise, Koji Mizoguchi (2013) has developed a regional textbook on Japan organized according to environment, social hierarchies, governance, monuments, and networks, all topics of interest throughout the world and representing a new look at where these features, including gender, can be studied within a culture that identifies itself as both separate and yet linked across Asia. Most recently, Bryan Miller's (2024) book on the Xiongnu pays attention to regional archaeological settings with the aid of textual accounts, results of scientific testing, and ethnographic parallels of family histories and societal order. Natasha Fijn's (2011) sensitive account of the fluid gendered division of labor and leadership among pastoralists in central Mongolia offers a gendered picture as a guide.

1.3 Sections of This Element

This Introduction describes common features of scholarship across East Asia and discusses where we think the study of gender stands today while keeping in mind and bringing to the fore the effects of the sociopolitical and historical settings in which analyses currently are being rendered. We note differing approaches to archaeological investigation and the attendant methodological decisions that have guided and shaped what is studied, especially gender.

Although there are clear problems with organizing our discussions according to modern national boundaries, in what follows we have done so because we think it gives a clear picture of how the issue is currently being discussed and points out the need for future study that crosses those modern national boundaries. Reconsideration of spatial divisions for ancient cultures in the future will hopefully be attempted and, if so, they will certainly require collaboration. More robust understanding of how gender was positioned and what roles or functions it shaped in these societies will also require interdisciplinary thinking that has as one of its goals contextual and synthetic historical analysis. Finally, we hope that what we have projected here will push scholarship on gender forward in the future.

2 Current Research

2.1 People's Republic of China (PRC)

2.1.1 Nationalism and Chinese Archaeology

In his statement about Chinese archaeology on September 9, 2020, the PRC president Xi Jinping made clear the significance of knowledge of the past to his contemporary program of "National Rejuvenation" (民族复兴 *Minzu fuxing*). He specified that archaeology must be built with Chinese characteristics and in a Chinese style that will allow better understanding of the long and profound Chinese civilization. He claimed that the Chinese civilization has unique cultural genes and that its developmental history was rooted in the land of China and its communications with other civilizations in the world (Xi 2020). Of course, this means that archaeology could be a focus for increased national attention and funding if its claimed purpose were to search for a "Chinese" civilization. Although expressed within contemporary political ambitions, this view is not new in Chinese intellectual history. In a later statement on October 30, 2023, Xi called for China's women to start a "new trend of family" as the nation grapples with declining birth rates and an aging population. Doing a good job in women's work is not only related to women's own development, he said, but also related to "family harmony, social harmony, national development and national progress" (Xinhua 2023). This call for a focus on older Chinese ideals, although aimed at unifying China today, follows a model that has shaped current analyses of its historical societies, including those about gender.

The study of men and women in Chinese historic and even prehistoric societies most often has been defined within a traditional paradigm that has perpetuated established views about gendered roles. For instance, one of the most conspicuous renderings of those conventional views about Chinese women's roles appeared in the *Biographies of Women* (列女傳 *Lie Nü Zhuan*) compiled by the Han 汉 scholar Liu Xiang 刘向 (77–6 BCE) and has been reiterated and commented on again and again over the centuries. The essays generalize thinking about suitable roles based primarily on the lives of elite women and men within Chinese imperial society. Does this repeated attention to "proper" behavior suggest that women were consistently "misbehaving," thus provoking the need to reiterate the standards in order to remind women of "suitable" behavior? Perhaps.

These traditional ideas guide thinking even today in some circles. For instance, the *Biographies of Women* was compiled by a male Confucian scholar, and the essays outline "appropriate" roles and behavior for elite women, both positive and negative. Those texts not only were revived and commented on in Chinese and transported to Korea and Japan over the centuries but have also been translated in part and in full several times into Western languages. Probably the most influential version known in the West is by a Jesuit priest named Albert O'Hara (1971), so there is the possibility of an overlay of Catholic points of view transmitted there as well. This is not the place to examine the subtleties of modern translations, except to say that a fruitful avenue of research would be to examine the male-centered choice of transmitted and translated words as they have affected interpretation of behavior, especially that of females now and in the past.[5]

For instance, as O'Hara translates them, the original scrolls are titled:

1. Correct Deportment of Mothers (母 儀 傳)
2. The Virtuous and Wise (賢 明 傳)
3. The Benign and Wise (仁 智 傳)
4. The Chaste and Obedient (貞 順 傳)
5. The Principled and Righteous (節義傳)
6. Those Able in Reasoning and Understanding (辯 通 傳)
7. The Pernicious and Depraved (孼 嬖 傳)

[5] Poo looked for and made subtle readings of the male vs. female voice in this text and several others (Poo 2018: 186–206).

What the texts affirm is that Chinese (or Asian) women (including those in Korea and Japan) were limited in the roles and professions open to them, and the ways in which they could use the clout and advantages afforded them were most often as a result of natal family influence/protections. Those relationships were/are described through the lens of Confucian ideas about individuals knowing their place in the natural order as governed by hierarchical social relations such as filial piety – ruler to ruled, father to son, husband to wife, elder brother to younger brother, friend to friend, and so forth – that explain behavior as a matter of proper social status. Such views of men and women became canonical and have loomed large in the search for archaeologically rendered debris as evidence of past behaviors.

Geng Chao 耿超 (2014) has argued, for instance, that hierarchy in relation to socioeconomic class was displayed in the burial furniture of the principal wives of the marquises of Jin (晋侯) (tenth to eighth century BCE) at Beizhao, Quwo, Shanxi Province (山西曲沃北赵村) during the Western Zhou dynasty (西周). Couples were placed in joining tomb chambers and the noble wives were treated in death with roughly similar elaborate burial furniture as their husbands in order to show other members of society their power and high status (Geng 2014).

Relationships of women to their fathers, brothers, and husbands as reported in the *Biographies of Women* were apparently seen as a matter of social convention rather than necessarily of second-class status, a point that is often confused in modern discussions of gender about women regardless of class. Marriage was critical to binding two families and, beyond them, broader groups of families together politically and economically, for instance. Women married into the "job of linking" and could often work in subtle ways to help the family succeed in its enterprises to undermine the efforts of other families.[6] As reviewed by Yong Ying 雍颖 (2004, 2006) in the same cemetery of the Jin State as just discussed, combined readings of archaeological materials and contemporary inscriptional records of political relations between neighboring peoples led her to conclude that the graves of the principal wives of the marquises of the state of Jin not only marked cross-cultural and interethnic bonds between former enemies but also showed that the principal wives' tombs toward the end of that period were more elaborately outfitted than those of their husbands. The increased embellishment of these women's tombs, Yong suggested, had to do with waning power of the Jin and their attempt to regain political and military power through showing favored status to women from influential natal families

[6] Thanks to Professor H. Anne Weis who is working on a case of elite Greek women's conventional roles for helping us think this through.

where an alliance could provide such a boost. The diplomatic role of these women, therefore, was noteworthy and primary, but this sort of task was not in the forefront of written historical texts and has only quite recently surfaced, especially when scholars have made use of inscriptional as well as archaeological evidence that expose variations in the prescribed Confucian social order (see, e.g., Yong 2004, 2006; Khayutina 2017, 2014; Kinney 2018, 2014; Sun 2021).

Archaeological investigations, and especially those that provide scientific testing of archaeological materials and human remains, clearly have the data that could challenge those paradigms but have been shaped by and effected modern political, social, and even economic history. If one takes the establishment of the People's Republic of China as a case in point, its socialist ideology could be seen as a catalyst for change in gendered behavior. Equivalency in roles for men and women was sought, at least in theory. Past models were put into narratives and displayed all over China, for instance, in the eight model ballets of the 1960s (Wilcox 2019: 119–155). There women joined the military and sought freedom from the bondage of servitude, all while still learning from their male counterparts (Linduff 2022). Missteps of the past were derided as inglorious and worthy of punishment as well as served to suggest and foster various changes in gendered roles. Yet still old views that sexualized women persisted in these performances where even military uniforms on the "liberated" women clung tight to their bodies, for instance (Linduff 2022). Even so, attempts by the government to urge gender equality and the rise of the Chinese feminist movement certainly allowed more women to become archaeologists more readily than in the past and to look for topics about the social roles of men and women (JUIAF 2008; Zhang 2008; NUAC 2010; Pu 2018; Yang 2021) as will be outlined in the following section.

2.1.2 Historical Perspective

As the analyses of the secondary literature on what is being called "gendered archaeology" will show, a rich array of archaeological, ethnographic, and textual sources has been drawn upon in researching women and gender in prehistoric and early historic periods of China. Included as evidence are mortuary assemblages, excavated and received texts, inscriptions, figurines, pictorial images, and occasionally ethnographic accounts. Some of the papers are ambitious in scope and investigate gender relations or themes such as gender ideology, gender roles and status, women and power in a complex society, and the notion of gendered intersecting identities among the elite. Often such topics are laced with the analysis of scientific testing of artifacts and human and animal remains and add a new feature for consideration of particular aspects of human health, movement from place to place, roles, and so on.

What appears to be in its infancy are discussions about the conceptualization of gender. The majority of studies (in China and elsewhere in East Asia) have focused on the "actions, status, or simply the presence of women [and/or men] in past societies" (Joyce and Claassen 1997: 1) and that is a beginning. In some studies, especially those that are based on the analysis of mortuary debris, gender tends to be equated with sex, often based on biologically sexed skeletons. The distinction between sex as based on observable biological differences and gender as a historically specific, cultural, and social construct is a concept not always evoked in favor of the reporting of either relevant scientifically based data on sex or attempts to discern heritage. Overall, there is a need for conceptual clarity for gender to be understood as a historically specific construction of identity that is fluid, mutable, and negotiated over the course of one's life, including at one's death (Bacus 2006: 633).

Before the 1980s, some interesting studies on gender were undertaken, especially by historians. These are reviewed by Linduff and Sun (2004: 3) where they are characterized as challenges to holistic views of such conventions as marriage, lineage, division of labor, and so forth. Based primarily on the rereading of texts, however, they do show a growing interest in gender studies in general. More recently, Du Jinpeng's 杜金鹏 study of gender relations in the Xia (夏) and Shang (商) periods makes use not only of historical texts but also of oracle bones and mythology (Du 1995: 93–133). The volume in which the article was published shows a very clear attempt to distinguish "male and female" behavior across Chinese dynastic history but makes more reference to ideological conceptions posited in texts than from evidence from archaeological data (Ma 1995).

Advocacy for gender studies in the United States and among students of China has added momentum to the growing interest both in the West and in China. The publication of edited volumes has provoked an uptick in interest in including studies beyond Europe and the United States. Clearly the pioneer in this was Sarah Nelson whose numerous and persistent publications allowed gender as reported in Asian contexts to enter the worldwide stage for debate (1990, 1991a, 1991b, 1995, 1996, 1997, 1998, 2002, 2003, 2006, 2008, 2016; see also Sections 2.1 and 2.2). Additionally, the first edited volume on gender and Chinese archaeology includes twelve papers that focus on mortuary analysis and covers the period from the late Neolithic through the Han dynasty (ca. 3000 BCE–200 CE) (Linduff and Sun 2004, 2006 [in Chinese]). The study of gendered identity as expressed in mortuary settings has been an effective avenue of research since there is no written documentation in the late

Neolithic period. For example, one of the papers examined the 804 burials excavated at the late Neolithic cemetery at Dadianzi 大甸子 in Inner Mongolia (内蒙古) (ca. 1600 BCE) and suggested that gender played a significant part in burial display at Dadianzi cemetery where artifacts appeared to mark societal inequality between males and females (Wu, J. M. 2004, 2006). The deceased males faced the habitation site and females face away from it, and statistical analysis of the burial goods conducted by (Mandy) Jui-man Wu 吳瑞滿 showed that sex and age, and also class, were reflected in the number, type, and location of burial goods. She used these results to reconstruct what these differences revealed about status and power relations across the Dadianzi society but was also able to show through the analysis of grave goods that some work was gendered by activity. Most adult males, for instance, engaged in hunting, fighting, and planting, based on the presence of axes, tools, and weapons in their tombs, while only females of lower status were weavers, based on the presence of spindle whorls only in female tombs with modest sets of grave goods. She also showed that male status was closely related to achievement as evidenced by the accumulation of nonlocal, fancy pottery, while female status was governed by a woman's marriage partner, although wealth could be obtained from both her natal family and her marriage. This analysis fine-tuned our understanding of the social structure of the society beyond the hierarchical tier system determined previously in the archaeological fieldwork of Shelach (1999). The use of statistical analysis on a particular cemetery has proven to be effective by others and more recent studies on the prehistoric period have adopted this method (Qiao 2014; Wang 2012; Wang and Zhang 2008; Yang and Ai 2022; Zhang 2020). Characteristic of many if not most of these analyses both in East Asia and beyond is their interdisciplinary approach, as, for example, with the use of statistical and art historical methods of analysis by Jui-man Wu. In addition, many focus on the analysis of a single cemetery presumably because that is the sort of data that are available but also because it yields, intentionally or not, some sense of community and its overall complexion.

Two conferences followed the publication of *Gender and Chinese Archaeology* (Linduff and Sun 2004, 2006 [in Chinese]) in China; the first at Jilin University in 2007 and the second held at Nanjing University in 2010 ("Woman's Archaeology and Woman's Heritage") (女性考古与女性遗产). In these contexts, we see attempts to identify the interdependency between gender ideology and power, status, family, social roles, and cultural identity. These essays and meetings created a foundation for further studies, notwithstanding criticism of such efforts as needing more clarity on gender as a historically constructed category of human behavior (Brumfiel 2007: 237–242). This has proven a very difficult task in the majority of studies of gender, most of which come from archaeologists in China. There the most exciting addition to the field has been the use of scientific testing of archaeological materials that provides certain evidence of sex such that how it is treated in burial might allow for an understanding of ideas about gender.

2.1.3 Methods and Issues Currently Applied to Gendered Analyses

Although research that takes on gendered social order has been undertaken by scholars outside of China using available published data, archaeological investigation has not always been aimed at discovering gendered behavior in survey and excavation programs at the outset. In reviewing the results of reported scientific testing such as AMS dating, DNA and genome analysis, strontium or stable isotope analysis, and others later in this Element, one can see that this sort of testing often refutes and brings into question conventional gendered paradigms so clearly outlined in ideological texts such as the *Biographies of Women* mentioned in Section 2.1.1. Roles of women and men throughout prehistoric and early historic times can and are suggested at the local level in many of these reports but the use of such data to seek out and document broader patterns of behavior, inconsistent as they may have been both with traditional views and across the ancient dynastic terrain, has not yet been systematically and synthetically accomplished.

Issues that Chinese archaeologists are currently addressing and reporting in their archaeological accounts include the following:[7]

1. Kinship (Wang 2012); marriage patterns (Geng 2013, 2014); ethnic and racial composition (Wang 2012) of China's early "civilizations."
2. Status and class structure (Zhang 2018; Sun 2019; Yu 2019; Zhang 2016).
3. Household work and division of labor (Qiao 2014).
4. Political organization (Huang 2011; Chen et al. 2013; Geng 2013, 2014; Li 2015).
5. Health of populations (Wang 2012) and nutrition (Zhang 2015; Zhang and Li 2014; Zhang et al. 2022).
6. Migration of peoples and ethnic composition (or "integration") of populations (Zhang 2015).

Such social issues have been addressed especially through the analysis of burial patterns and assessment of such features as sex, age, and "ethnic" background. Artifact analysis has been aided by more and more precise measuring techniques

[7] The literature that purports to study or at least include analyses of gender is extensive. Not all is listed here, but representative articles are noted that will lead readers to other studies.

and increasingly sophisticated analysis of use wear of weapons, for instance (Sun 2019); differences in clothing (including cross-dressing, see Tang 2021), production tools, ornaments, and so on aligned with sexes have been applied in order to explain differing identities of the deceased (Sun 2019; Zhang 2020; Fang 2021; Wang S. 2021). It is worth mentioning here that, although Tang Xiaowen 唐晓雯 (2021) uses evidence dating from the seventh-century tomb of a princess of the Tang dynasty (唐, 618–907 CE) and later than that covered in this Element, a case is made that the deceased woman dressed in men's clothing was a show of resistance to traditional feudal etiquette. Perhaps the more overt display of the changing social status of women in the multiethnic upper classes of the Tang were the figurines and paintings of women riding astride, playing polo, and accompanying male entourages on diplomatic occasions found in tombs of the elite throughout the Tang (Zhang 2019).

Many of the articles listed in this section include studies of human skeletal remains based on paleodemography (death and age structures, population growth) and paleopathology, including stable isotope analysis of diet and health that shows results of prehistoric women in Inner Mongolia Autonomous Region (IMAR), for instance, who ate more millet and males who ate more meat (Zhang and Li 2014; Zhang et al. 2022).

Cranial morphology and paleoethnology, body size estimation and behavior reconstruction, population mixing and male vs. female DNA lines of descent, and many others are also topics of special interest and now are aided by scientific studies. Because of the availability and use of these methods, the nature of gender studies worldwide, including in China, is changing. Numerous related studies of human remains have been conducted by a group of scholars headed by Professor Zhu Hong 朱泓 and his graduate students at Jilin University. For instance, Zhang Qun 张群 focused on a collection of basic information for further understanding the social structure, health status, division of labor, funeral customs, and marriage patterns of the population during the Han dynasty (Zhang 2018). By making use of paleopathological research, others have discovered and analyzed dental diseases (Wang and Zhang 2008; Zhou and Li 2010; Wang 2012; Zhao 2013; Shen et al. 2021) as well as ritual practices of dental extraction (Li 2021; Shen et al. 2021). Yet others are conducting targeted genetic DNA studies that provide information on phylogenetic lines of descent (Zhang 2005; Jia 2006) and evolution of humans, including evidence of the Rui 芮 group, who were found to be of mixed heritage and to have died earlier than those in the Western Zhou regional control group (Zheng 2012). Recently, multivariate statistical methods have been used to study topics comparatively, including sex, age, height, and bone pathology (Jia 2006; Wang 2014; Zhou 2014; Shen et al. 2021; Nie 2022; Sun L 2013); demography and ethnology (Zhao 2013); and paleopathology, nutrition, and skull morphology to determine "race and ethnicity" (Yang and Ai 2022), including statistical analysis of burial goods and gender. The most recent methodological experimentation is with geometric morphometry (Liu 2021; Wang 2021) that looks at a history of physiognomy developed in the pre-Qin (先秦) period and uses a collection of approaches to provide a mathematical description of biological forms according to geometric definitions of their size and shape. How to connect this to gendered ideas and behavior awaits.

A closer look at one of these papers gives some idea of the main foci, types of studies underway, and their significance nationally. Zhao Yongsheng 赵永生, while a PhD student at Jilin University, focused on analyses of human bones in the Mogou cemetery in Lintan, Gansu (甘肃临潭磨沟墓地) (Zhao 2013). Anthropological and archaeological evidence from there suggests that before the Qin and Han dynasties the broader region hosted multiple different source populations with morphometric and technological connections to both Western and Eastern Eurasia. The Mogou cemetery dates from the Qijia culture (齐家文化) period (ca. 2200–1600 BCE) and is in the region where and time period when incipient metal production technologies emerged that were eventually transferred into the heartland of early dynastic China. Such technologies became central and unifying components of dynastic state spiritual and political power (Flad 2023). Dating at the cusp of the transition from the Neolithic to the Bronze Age and the establishment of the first "Chinese" state, the authors propose that research on the "ethnic" attributes (as defined by Zhao 赵) of the Mogou residents is of great interest to the question about what "racial" groups contributed to the formation of Chinese civilization. Demographic, ethnologic, paleopathological, and nutrition studies were carried out and found that the men and women at the Mogou site belonged to a mixed Asian Mongolian race that contributed as a source population to modern North China residents of the northern Han ethnicity (汉族). What the nature of that ethnic, demographic, or "racial" mixing was and whether it was based on the movement of women, for instance, is an issue that is not addressed. Further review of male vs. female nutrition and of the wear on bones would, perhaps, also offer insight into such issues as division and types of labor as well as status of the sexes.

The potential for comparative and synthetic studies is clearly possible as the work has been conducted all across northern and western regions as well as parts of southern China. This has not yet been attempted, nor have the collective databases been constructed to make that work possible, as far as we know. The summation of this research, even after our review here, leads to confirmation of differing lifestyles and cultural (often called "ethnic" [种族的] in the Chinese literature) backgrounds across and throughout prehistory and early dynastic China, as well as nonuniform roles for sexes (Zhang 2018).

Perhaps one of the most vexing issues in these studies is the continued confidence placed in morphological analysis to define ethnicity, culture, and sex, as well as many other topics (Sun 2013). It is a common foundation of study across East Asia and in Eurasia, where the Russians also continue to use such methods. Although Franz Boas' paper on the plasticity of human cranial morphology has been widely cited for decades and calls into question results about human lineages based on the assessment of head types (Boas 1912),[8] morphological studies remain current across China and East Asia. Even though the numerous factors that can affect craniometric variation such as genetics, environment, population interaction and breeding – and thus gene flow – are known in East Asia, and genetic testing is more common than ever, morphological measurements are regularly conducted and included in reports but not always by cross-checking previous reasoning about their efficacy in the face of new scientific data. This is evident in a study made by Hou Kan 侯侃 for his dissertation at Jilin University in 2017 (Hou 2017). Using sophisticated research methods on human skeletons, Hou caried out paleodemographic, paleopathological, skull morphology and paleoethnological testing, and body size estimations on a population from pre-Qin tombs in Higher Education Park in Yuci, Shanxi (山西榆次高校园区). Hou showed that cranial morphology showed no significant difference between males and females and that they there were of mixed heritage, but his discovery of degenerative bone disease and other anomalies in the osteological evidence was not analyzed in relation to gendered behavioral patterns.

Another perplexing issue that surfaces in the review of this literature is the uncritical and inconsistent use of terms such as "ethnicity" (民族 minzu) vs. "race" (种族 zhongzu) vs. "nationality" (国籍 guoji). In spite of the research that has shown that gene pools across Asia were formed through the mixing of lines of descent and the knowledge that genetic structure does not determine "ethnicity" or gender roles and that they are culturally constructed notions, the search to explain the formation of the "Chinese" civilization has frequently turned to determinations of "us and them," or attempts to define what ethnicities or races constituted Chinese vs. non-Chinese groupings. Scientific testing of DNA alone, for instance, has upended reasoning based on simple observations

[8] During the nineteenth century, anthropologists in the West argued that skull capacity equated directly with intelligence, arguing that because the brains of Caucasians were larger, they were smarter by comparison to Native Americans and people of African descent. In the early twentieth century another feature, cranial index, was proposed as a discerning feature of races and ethnic groups, and the shape of the human skull was thought to indicate criminality. Boas' (1912) paper countered these racist and colonial views. More recently, many other forms of analysis, such as genetic testing, have been developed that discern with more certainty the backgrounds and links among human beings. See, for instance, the review of the issue by S. J. Gould (1981).

such as "foreign" artifacts or burial patterns that have led to an assumed background and sex of the deceased. Marriage and lifestyle patterns, known to have historically and intentionally joined outsiders with insiders, have been the subject of many historical tales and were poignantly related in the poetry preserved in the "Eighteen Songs on a Nomad Flute" (胡笳十八拍). That account of a marriage between a Xiongnu 匈奴 leader and a Chinese woman in the second century CE flaunts a cultural dichotomy between the "steppe and the sown" from the Chinese point of view (see Rorex 1974). Some contend that, in addition to the "ethnic" or "racial" stereotyping that informs the story and the emotional attitude of the female protagonist, the poems may have been told via a "male" voice (Poo 2018: 201–203). That the notions of race, ethnicity, and sex vs. gender are culturally constructed as they might be understood in Western anthropological circles is beginning to be debated in East Asian publications (Qin 2021).

Nevertheless, even without comparative analysis, what one can see in the testing is a very diverse population across China in the late Neolithic, Bronze, and Iron ages. Moreover, this and other research clearly show that the Central Plain was not the only core, and populations were shifting around and mixing. That mixing was foretold in several of the papers in the volume *Gender and Chinese Archaeology* published in 2004 (Linduff and Sun 2004, 2006). Xiaolong Wu, for example, showed that the burial orientation, location, contents, and size in the cemetery at Maoqinggou, IMAR (内蒙古毛庆沟) displayed differences in male and female status and background (Wu XL 2004; see also Linduff 2006, 2008). That intersection of people suggests even superficially that differing ideas about gender roles across culture, class, age, and geographic location are in need of rethinking. Knowledge of the genetic background of a person or people does not, of course, necessarily link to roles in the ancient world. Genetic studies might link to Xi Jinping's call for "national rejuvenation" and provoke rethinking about the heritage of the men and women who contributed to the formation of Han nationality and how that might be further determined archaeologically. As has already been shown, the political role of women in marriage was one way that the population was diversified and could give women added status and power.

2.1.4 Future Studies of Gender

Perhaps most interesting and challenging will be clarification of the difficult issue of how to discern constructed views of gender from archaeological debris. Placing gender as a central research focus, as opposed primarily to identifying differences in sexes, would certainly help scholars test and retest their own assumptions as well as conclusions. Such questions would include the following: How can gender be discovered and analyzed in archaeological investigations? Can ethnicity be discerned from either archaeological or morphological study? What role should received texts (from the male perspective) play in archaeological studies? What is the male vs. female voice in received and/or inscriptional texts as well as in secondary literature on gender today? How and who can build cross-province/project/nation databases on sex-based information? How can greater use of historical context drive and explain gender differences? What synthetic studies are possible now about gender distinctions? What sorts of collaborations would join scientific data with historical contexts? What can be learned from the analysis of previous studies on gender in other language publications?

2.2 Korea

2.2.1 Sociocultural and Political Factors in the Study of Gender

As is the case all across East Asia, the study of gender in Korea has been affected by persistent, if somewhat changing, traditional sociocultural attitudes and intellectual movements, together with the rise of nationalism in the face of global issues focused on human rights, including equal rights for women and minorities. Interestingly, and despite the Eurocentric assumptions about the origins of feminism, early twentieth-century Korea witnessed a vibrant and radical feminist movement that called out sexual harassment in the workplace and spoke openly about female sexual pleasure. During Japanese colonial rule (1910–1945), an all-women anti-colonial organization called Rose of Sharon (샤론의 장미; 沙龍的玫瑰) was established in 1927 and included nationalists, socialists, Christians, and Buddhists. Its goal was to promote women's status and the national independence movement in Korea (Barraclough 2021). This movement brought attention to gender issues if only to be squashed under the further Japanese colonization of northeast Asia. Even so, issues of gender were not forgotten. The rise of democratization, from the end of military rule in the late 1980s, was actively shaped by women as well as men and might have been expected to have delivered greater benefits to half of the population, although gains have been slow to arrive.

Today, South Korea's feminist renaissance has repivoted narratives of female emancipation (Barraclough 2021) and a more ambitious and comprehensive analysis of the systemic barriers impeding the flourishing and advancement of women has begun to redefine society's notion of democracy, equality, and prosperity. This period spawned a great deal of research that proposed feminist points of view and sought to discover and bring to the fore the history of women throughout Korean history (see, among others, Cheong 1998; Choi 1986; Kim 1976; Lee 2008; Maloney 2004; Haboush 2008; Nahm 1989). It also saw the founding of the first modern Korean educational institution exclusively for women, Ewha Womans University (이화여자대학교; 梨花女子大學) 1910 to present (Ewha n.d.; Park 1990; Kim et al. 2000). This movement also brought greater recognition of the possibility and lack of study of gender in the ancient past in northeast Asia.

Although much of this effort has been given to rethinking gendered labor discrimination and segregated labor market and economic opportunities in the late twentieth century in South and North Korea, as in other parts of the world, those who write on Korean archaeology consistently lament the lack of women in certain professions, including archeology (Nelson 2013). It was as a result of the efforts of key scholars who pursued gendered research that endeavors have emerged to tease out possible evidence of differentiated roles of men and women in antiquity from the excavated inventories and literary accounts (Matsumoto 2010; Nelson 1991a, 1993, 2002, 2008a, 2013; Piggott 1999).

Archaeological research in Korea has so far focused on categories of inquiry such as periodization issues for the entire period from the Paleolithic era to the Silla (신라; 新羅) kingdom and analyses of lifeways and their change during that time period; the rise of agriculture; chronologies and refinement of dating systems pertaining to the periods listed above; the peopling of the peninsula; and the emergence and development of technologies, including especially the very early production of ceramics and the subsequent making of metal, glass, and stone artifacts whether for utilitarian or ritual use.[9] Most archaeological efforts have documented burials, with a few exceptions such as the broadscale excavation of Jungdo, Chuncheon (중도춘천; 中島春川) – an effort that has become a primary source of information on early Korean ways of life (Meller 2016; Lee 2018) that is now threatened by the construction of a large Legoland installation on the site. The largest prehistoric site in Korea excavated since 1945, it has revealed, for instance, continuous habitation and funerary data dating from the Neolithic period to the Joseon dynasty (조선; 朝鮮 1392–1897). Across this vast expanse of time, the role of gender was not often a crucial topic for these researchers, while instead the effort fulfilled desires to document linear accounts of Korean cultural and political history.

Efforts to focus attention on archaeological research in Korea worldwide, however, have been aided by publication projects such as the major compilation sponsored by the Early Korea Project in the Korea Institute at Harvard

[9] The bibliography for these periods and technologies is vast. For an overview, see Nelson (1993). For an extensive bibliography on Korean archaeology, see "Korean History: A Bibliography," compiled by Kenneth Robinson: www.hawaii.edu/korea/biblio/archaeology.html.

University edited by Mark Byington and written by local Korean archaeologists (Byington 2008, 2009, 2012). Importantly, this Korea project and efforts by Korean archaeologists in general, along with Sarah Nelson's 1993 *Archaeology of Korea*, have brought attention to a little-known prehistory of Korea to those outside of Korea and urged further study in the peninsula. Journals, as in most Asian nations, continue to report finds in great numbers in local languages.

2.2.2 The Genetic Composition of Ancient Korean Populations

With the sophisticated testing for genome sequences, Korean scientists have embraced the study of their own ancestry across prehistory up to the present day. For instance, Kim Jungeum and his team have endeavored to provide a long view of admixtures of populations to include genomes from Pleistocene hunter-gathers to Iron Age farmers in the Korean peninsula (Kim et al. 2020). Their research shows a gradual mixture of two major genetic components from East Siberia and Southeast Asia, including South China, but they do not speculate on how or why those migrations took place.

With this further understanding of the movement of Asian populations, scholarship on early Korean political history has increased. For instance, ancient kingdoms on the Korean peninsula are now recognized to have played a major role in the geopolitics of early state formation in northeastern Eurasia even though information about sites in North Korea cannot at this time be incorporated into the picture. The excavation of Tomb 98 at Gyeongju (경주; 慶州), the capital of the ancient kingdom of Silla (57 BCE–935 CE), shows intersection with the mainland with items in burial of gold and jade (Kim and Pearson 1977; Kim 1982; Nelson 2003: 80) where Nelson argues leadership was in the hands of the queen (Nelson 2003). In yet another example, however, the domestication of horses that occurred in Mongolia has recently been argued to have been responsible for the movement of these animals across northern Asia and into the heartland of China (Miller and Brosseder 2017), Korea, and eventually Japan. Again, might these assembled excavated materials be mined for information on gender?

Although the social dimensions of early Korean societies have been addressed recently, even that activity has often skirted the issue of gender and its role in the formation and maintenance of Korean society. But several topics have emerged and have received attention:

1. Gender in belief systems such as shamanism (Nelson 2008, 2016).
2. Gender and social order – household archaeology and women as potters in the Neolithic period (Nelson 2003, 2013).

3. Gender of rulership in ranked societies in Korea in the Bronze Age and early statehood (Nelson 2003, 2008, 2016).

2.2.3 Gender in Belief Systems

The earliest extant Korean documents, in the form of folktales, describe the origin of the nation, the ruling dynastic clan, and other consanguineal groups. The myth of Tangun (단군; 檀君) is the oldest foundation myth of Korea and it has had continuous authority in Korean politics and nationalism for more than a thousand years (Grayson 2015: 253). It credits a son of Heaven named Tangun and his wife (who had been a bear) as the progenitors of the Korean people. Other early records mention goddesses of mountains as the mother of an early queen (Nelson 1995). All probably were manifestations of animistic spirits who could be either male or female, but this myth sparked or was provoked by a belief in the power of the couple to generate the whole of the Korean population (Nelson 2013: 340).

Depictions of gendered persons invoke the notion that women were spirit leaders from the earliest recorded periods on the peninsula. We know that shamanism in Korea today is almost exclusively practiced by women (Kendall 1996) and this observation has suggested that the same was so in Korean prehistory. For instance, in pecked rock art in Korea dated to the Bronze Age Okladnikov has identified fishing scenes where heart-shaped faces, as on masks worn by females and known from ethnographic parallels, are comparable to the same on painted pottery from the third millennium BCE. He interpreted them as shamanic and suggests that these humanlike images are female (Okladnikov 1981). Although fishing is a known occupation of early inhabitants of the peninsula, no direct archaeological evidence shows definitively that this was a gendered occupation (Nelson 2013: 338).

Tombs of Koguryo (고구려; 高句麗), dated between the fourth and seventh centuries, show richly attired women as wives of the major tomb occupant or as servants who are depicted in smaller stature than the high-status women. In the Shijia cemetery (石家), Tomb 1, in Fushun 撫順, Liaoning 遼寧, on the other hand, the main occupant of the tomb is female. The murals in that tomb show a procession of women turned toward a larger female, presumably a depiction of the tomb occupant (Li 2016; Nelson 2013: 339). In other tombs, both male and female servants bring food and drink to a couple in a tent (Perrin 2010). Other images clearly show women dressed as shamans and yet others as apsara in Buddhist pictures (Nelson 2013). These depictions give a glimpse of established roles for men and women and document social ordering with elite women depicted as subordinate to the deceased male, as singled out for independent interment, and as spiritualized personages. Such images have been used to suggest the existence of gendered social hierarchies both with regard to men and among women as part of complex societies (Nelson 2013).

2.2.4 Gender and Social Order: Household Archaeology

Households anywhere are fundamental social units of sedentary societies, and when research is shaped to discern their features, gender could appear as a topic for investigation. Current efforts to design projects and carry out investigation of households in the archaeological record are underway (Lee and Bale 2016; Kim 2011) and might be expanded to include gender as a feature of analysis. Artifacts most often come from burials but occasionally are found and reported in household settings, where groups of certain items are speculated to denote gender roles. Pearson, for instance, suggests that pottery, especially cooking pots in early prehistoric settings, served activities centered around women and children and were probably produced by women (Pearson 2006).

When tied to an interest in documenting the emergence of social inequality, studies could create interest in change in gender roles especially in the Incipient to Middle Mumun periods (무문; 無文) ca. 1500–400 BCE). Across that period, for instance, the investigators have shown how large, rectangular multi-family dwellings were abandoned in the Middle Mumun (ca. 850–400 BCE) to accommodate smaller, single-family structures assumed to be kin. That has signaled Lee and Bale to suggest greater competition among households and increased complexity overall. The attendant aspect of this change was the emergence of incipient elites (Lee and Bale 2016). This change in house morphology and segmented spaces is thought to result from subsistence changes that required a different kind of labor organization and the shift from a more homogeneous society to one that was hierarchically or heterogeneously ordered (Grier and Kim 2012; Kim 2011, 2015; Lee and Bale 2016). Although these careful descriptions and analyses of spatial ordering and change in economies expose modifications in social order and have the potential for locating gendered tasks, they have so far remained mute on gender issues.

Scientific testing of human bone has very recently exposed dietary indications of social differentiation. Results from isotopic investigation of skeletal remains from the later Proto-Three Kingdoms period (ca. 80 BCE–395 CE), for instance, has provided information on diet. Overall, most animal food from the diets of the Imdang (임당; 林堂) burials (Gyeongsan City 경산시; 慶山市), South Korea have been shown to derive from subsistence hunting of game birds and terrestrial herbivores. Marine fish and shellfish from coastal regions showed that these were intentionally imported. Interestingly, the isotopic variation within individuals supports the notion that ancient Imdang society was stratified with a strict system of food supply and demand. In the tombs, no differences in diets were found among the elites based on sex, age, or burial type. However, there were significant differences in the diets between elites and retainers, even though they were buried in the same graves. Very different food consumption patterns within the same community were found and showed that the social position of individuals was much more important than the sex and age of an individual (Choy et al. 2021).

2.2.5 Female Leadership

This topic is informed variously through textual study, especially in early states, and ethnographic parallels and less frequently on excavated materials. Noting that nearly all studies on shamanism concede that shamans are women, Nelson has posited that the "importance of understanding gender and shamanism is made clear when discussing shamanism and leadership" (Nelson 2013: 338; Nelson 2008).

Although many have reviewed the implicit universality of assumptions about nuclear family, male dominance, and gendered labor in intermediate societies as ubiquitous (Ames 1995, 2007; Pyburn 2004: 5), after the establishment of states, both in Japan and Korea, there is documented female leadership. This is found in the reigning queens of the Silla kingdom centered at Gyeongju ([Sŏndŏk 선덕여왕 善德女王 r. 632–647]; [Chindŏk 진덕여왕 眞德女王, or Chindok 진덕왕, 眞德王 r. 647–654]; [Chinsŏng 진성여왕, 眞聖女王 r. 887–849]). Called "female kings," they were part of a social system that is described with endogamous ranking. Women were eligible for leadership roles until the fifth century when patrilineal descent became the rule (Nelson 1991).

Knowledge of women among the leadership comes from the undisturbed Silla-date mounded tombs excavated beginning in the 1930s. Excavated in 1971 at Hwangnam Daejong (황남대종; 皇南大塚) (Kim and Lee 1975; Kim and Pearson 1977) were two overlapping tombs, a type known in both Silla and Kaya (가야; 加倻) territories. The larger of these tombs contained the trappings of leadership – a golden crown and other elaborate embellishments including a golden belt, glass beads, and jades. It has consistently been attributed to a female leader, whereas the earlier and smaller tomb was outfitted with weaponry and assigned to a male. Thus far there is no queen listed in the written documents of the same period as this large tomb, perhaps suggesting that coleaders might have been possible as was the case in Kofun (고분; 古墳) Japan (Piggott 1999). The existence of female leaders has been proposed by many, especially when considering the elaborate grave goods and the size of the female tomb at Hwangnam Daejong (Sasse 2001; Nelson 1991, 1993, 2002, 2013; Bunker 1978).

2.2.6 Future Considerations

Many questions suggested by excavated materials in the Korean peninsula still await careful and thoughtful interpretation, including those about gender. If incorporated into theoretical modeling, for instance, household archaeological investigations might include more scientific testing of human remains for sex identification, for gender-specific issues of diet, health, movement of peoples, division of labor, and kinship, and for other social structures, state development, and ideology. The scientific know-how is clearly available, and its more extensive use will lead to more nuanced and sophisticated interpretations of gender in Korea. Current discussions about the ceramic industry in northeast Asia as one of the earliest in the world, for instance, would be greatly enhanced if the sex of the potters and food preparers could be discerned. Likewise, traditional myths such as those that promote women as gatherers and men as hunters, that align the goddess hypotheses with early leadership, and that assume that warriors were all male may also be replaced with more refined models that would seek out actual gendered behavior and begin to tell a more human story of Korean prehistory and bring that history further into conversation with other narratives worldwide.

2.3 Japan

2.3.1 Japanese Archaeology and Gender Studies

As in other Asian nations, prevalent intellectual traditions, national funding and restrictive issuance of field permits have affected the goals of archaeological investigation in Japan in modern times, even among Japanese nationals. Archaeology has been positioned to serve traditional historical narratives and to promote the current notion of national identity, ideology, and cultural heritage (Ikawa-Smith 1980, 2002: 324). The study of women in ancient history in Japan began in the 1930s, yet gendered archaeology has been restricted to only a few researchers (Matsumoto and Mitsumoto 2022: 143). As Ikawa-Smith and Habu point out, studies of women in ancient Japan were initially written by Japanese feminist historians who contributed major work focused on gendered roles and positions, especially those of women, that were often based largely on textual accounts (Ikawa-Smith and Habu 2002: 324). This would include, for example, the inaugural volume of the journal *Sōgō Josei-shi-ken* (*Annual Review of Women's History* 総合女性史研), edited by the Sōgō Joseishi Kenkyukai

(Society for Research on Women's History 総合女性史学会), which was published by the University of Tokyo Press in 1983. Not surprisingly, however, the study of gender in archaeological settings in Japan was inspired by feminist studies in the West during the 1980s (Conkey and Spector 1984) and has been led by Japanese female archaeologists since the mid 1990s (Fujimura 1996, 1998; Matsumoto 1998; Ikawa-Smith and Habu 2002).

Gender perspectives have provided a new way to look at ancient societies even though modern concepts about women's roles sometimes have been uncritically applied to ancient families. Matsumoto Naoko 松本直子 made clear in 2017 the danger of projecting modern concepts of gender roles onto ancient societies and how that might lead to the misinterpretations of ancient family behavior. For instance, the public is shown a diorama of a pit house of the Yayoi period (ca. 300 BCE–300 CE) in the Osaka Prefectural Museum of Yayoi Culture (大阪府立弥生文化博物館) that depicts a family dinner scene with a father, a mother, two children, and dogs. In this presentation, a woman kneels to serve a meal to the men. The female archaeologist Hishida Junko 菱田淳子 criticized this reinterpretation of an ancient family because there is no archaeological data to support that view (Matsumoto 2017: 179). Matsumoto suggested that the intention of the museum was to show that stone tools and earthenware are difficult to understand by themselves, so the exhibition was meant to lead the audience to understand this activity in relation to behavior in modern life (Matsumoto 2017: 179–180). Matsumoto concluded that academic research should be conducted based firmly on data and suggests that exhibitions should invite viewers to think more critically about gender roles in ancient societies.

Research support for female archaeologists has been crucial for the study of gender in archaeology. Japanese female scholars point out that the research environment for them is limited (Ikawa-Smith and Habu 2002: 328–332), and Matsumoto and Mitsumoto (2022) mention two main reasons for the limited number of studies of gender in archaeology in Japan: (1) It is hard to challenge traditional views about women's roles in current society, and (2) archaeology has served historical narratives and emphasized their historical significance. Being a gender scholar is not appreciated, but female scholars in Japan are very enthusiastic about its study in archaeology and believe that their work has been fruitful, including studies on the Jōmon 縄文, Yayoi 弥生, and Kofun 古墳 periods and the emergence of LGBT-related queer archaeology (Mitsumoto 2019).

By reexamining women and their relations with men as expressed in the *Nihon shoki* (*Chronicles of Japan* 日本書紀), compiled by imperial decree in the eighth century, Gina Barnes (2006) has provided a text-based historical perspective on the study of gender in Japan. She suggests that elite women played multiple roles and had a more equal relationship with men in the protohistoric and early historic periods than in more recent premodern and modern periods. For example, females spoke as the oracles of male gods, even though in marriage women were commonly subordinated to males (Barnes 2006: 46). This sort of rethinking, even of the most traditional views expressed in official documents, could allow for a realignment of thinking about gender among students of ancient societies.

2.3.2 Archaeological Studies on Gender

As mentioned, since the mid 1990s some Japanese female scholars have been inspired by feminist and well-established gender studies in the West from the 1980s. Fujimura Junko 藤村純子 (1996) published the first article on gender and Japanese archaeology in the journal *Women's History* (女性史学) in 1996 and Matsumoto Naoko 松本直子 (1998) reported current studies on gender archaeology and published *The Annual Report of Women's Studies* (女性学年報) in 1998. Fujimura (1998) mentioned that many recent Western women's studies essays have been translated into Japanese. For example, in 1996 Ehrenberg's *Women in Prehistory* was translated into Japanese with the subtitle "Beginning of Gender Archaeological Studies," and a Japanese-language translation of related research was published around the same year. Additionally, Gerda Lerner's *The Creation of Patriarchy* was translated by Akiko Okuda and published in 1996 by Sanichi Publishing Co., Ltd. The availability of such studies allowed for the opening up of thinking about gender in Japan's past.

For instance, as early as 1998 Fujimura questioned the model of "men as hunters" and noted that the idea remains among academics because it reflects modern concepts in Japanese society and has been accepted as "normal" for men to obtain food while women stay at home taking care of children (Fujimura 1998: 72). Fujimura, however, found the Japanese translation of Elizabeth W. Barber's book (translated in 1996) *Women's Work: Ancient Lifestyle from the Viewpoint of Textiles* useful for her thinking about Japan.[10] Barber explained that her study of gender division in labor showed that men hunted, caught fish, took care of livestock, and went out of the community in search of luxury items such as black stones and shells, while women focused on self-sufficient agriculture and crafting including pottery-making and weaving balanced with childcare. Although Japanese scholarship upheld the notion that Jōmon agriculture was begun by "the retired hunters," Fujimura suggested that the rise in both

[10] Published in 1994, the title of this book was *Women's Work: The First 20,000 Years: Women, Cloth, and Society in Early Times*, which discussed issues about work from 6000 BCE to 2000 BCE in the early horticultural economy of southeastern Europe.

production of earthen wares and textiles and small-scale agriculture before the advent of large-scale irrigation for farming was done through division of labor and in conjunction with women (Fujimura 1998: 74). In addition, as Nelson (2013) pointed out in her study of coastal East Asia, some cultural patterns were shared across these regions, and across modern national boundaries. For example, similar kinship systems, the presence of shamans, depictions of gendered human beings, spirits and goddesses, and the gender of leadership were similar across northeast Asia. These well-noted patterns have emerged in studies on gender, although are limited depending on geopolitical tensions and archaeological culture definitions.

The study of early Japan has followed established prehistoric and historic political divisions and although transitions from one period to another are most often not uniform across the region, that framework has dominated archaeological thinking about Japan for decades, if not centuries. It brings already set linear notions of the process of change that do not always include the varying roles played by men and women and how that may have changed or why. Nevertheless, that is how research is structured currently and how it will be reported on here.

2.3.3 Pottery Figurines and Ornaments from the Jōmon Period

Aware of the abovementioned problems, Junko Habu joined aspects of Japanese and Anglo-American archaeological approaches and aimed at providing an overview of cultural complexity in Jōmon communities in her 2004 publication. Through examination of archaeological data from the Jōmon culture, she developed and demonstrated a model that included long-term developments toward cultural complexity and regional diversity in Jōmon. Because the study of gender in Japanese archaeology was in its infancy in the early 2000s, however, Habu pointed out that the limited discussions of gender in the study of early Japan was related to the small number of female archaeologists practicing in Japan and jobs in academic institutions were very limited for women (Habu 2004: 24–25).

Archaeological data from the Jōmon period do, however, include some artifacts uniquely suited to the study of gender. Ikawa-Smith and Habu (2002) published a general distribution outline of clay figurines across time and space and provided a critical review of the scholarship on them. They reported that more than 15,000 specimens have been collected. Because many of the figurines have gendered female attributes such as large breasts and hips or genital features, scholars have most often suggested that they represented mother goddesses and were associated with ritual activities. They urged archaeologists and scholars to explore gender-related questions as they believe that "Jōmon figurines have a great potential for informing us not only about myths and rituals surrounding women but also about their economic roles and the sociopolitical organization of Jōmon societies in general" (Ikawa-Smith and Habu 2002: 353).

In another type of study, Bausch (2019) examined the ornaments from five early Jōmon tombs (ca. 3400–2900 BCE) at the Odake Shell Midden in Toyama prefecture (Odake kaizuka, 小竹貝塚, 富山県), Japan (excavated in 2009–2010) while thinking about egalitarian hunter-gatherer societies. Challenging traditional interpretations of "male" vs. "female" ornaments, Bausch suggested that wearing ornaments was not regarded as crucial recognition of one's social status, association, job, or personal experiences but was associated with age. The data indicate that mature males and females were both buried with ornaments and suggest that adornments reflected the social value and significance of the reproductive role in egalitarian hunter-gatherer societies (Bausch 2019).

2.3.4 Food Consumption, Age, and Gender Roles in the Middle Jōmon Period

Matsumoto Naoko (2008) focused her studies on gendered archaeology in the Jōmon period and explained three important foci for study: gender roles in labor division; gender and power; and gender-related worldviews and symbols. In particular, she used excavated data from the Kitamura site (北村遺跡) (2000–1500 BCE), located in Nagano Prefecture (長野県), to discuss the complexity of gender roles in the Middle Jōmon associated with labor activities, age, and social responsibilities related to ritual activities. Matsumoto suggested that her analysis of the data from the Kitamura site challenges the stereotypical assumptions that males were hunters and females were gatherers. For example, quality stone tools, including stone hoes, grinding stones, and lithic axes found in female tombs were 1.1 times more prevalent than those in the male tombs and the number of grindstones found in female tombs was about 1.9 times more than that found in the male tombs of the same period. These suggest that both men and women worked on many different tasks (Matsumoto 2008: 139–140).

Gender roles have also been studied by analyzing food consumption. Archaeologists have used carbon and nitrogen isotopes and trace element testing to analyze human bones from the Kitamura sites to locate food habits (Akazawa et al. 1993). The overall results suggest that dietary habits were strongly dependent on C3 plants, and the proportion of the protein was lower probably because the Kitamura site is about 80 km away from the sea. Based on the perspective of sex and age, Matsumoto suggested that the carbon value of men is overall higher than that for women. However, the carbon value for women increased as they aged, bringing their totals closer to those for the men. Bone protein collagen took decades to be replaced, she argued, so changes in eating habits were not immediately reflected and it took time to show an average diet for a certain period such as that prior to death. The difference in consumption of cultivated plants such as Japanese foxtail millet, Japanese barnyard millet, and common millet, which are C4 plants, is the cause of the gender differences. Matsumoto suggested that in the early stages of farming cultivated plants were not staple food items but were a specialty only for ceremonial use (Matsumoto 2008: 140–142).

Age certainly was one of the key factors associated with societal roles. At the Kitamura site, there is a possibility that women participated in ceremonies only after reaching a certain age and thereby being able to partake of the special meal. Matsumoto suggested that if the gender differences in the carbon isotope ratios were derived from seafood consumption, it is possible that a group of men may have gone to the coast to fish during certain seasons, or that men mainly consumed seafood obtained through an exchange network. Given that many stone tools recovered were used for hunting and preparation of plants for cooking and were buried with women older than middle-age, women likely were centrally responsible for the food preparation and for hunting land animals in the vicinity of villages. It seems appropriate to think that the women who achieved certain social standing also consumed seafood brought to the village in some way (Matsumoto 2008: 141–142). Matsumoto concluded from the study of the Kitamura site that many men ate ceremonial food and consumed less of other food and that such men may have participated in ceremonies from a young age, while women participated only after reaching a certain age or position. The sex differences between the male burials containing wild boar tusks, jade accessories, and ritual meals may be interrelated, Matsumoto suggested. However, this is an interpretation based on eating habits and does not show that young women were excluded from rituals. In addition, it is necessary to examine the possibility that there were other rituals in which young women actively participated, but that hypothesis would have to be examined using additional data (Matsumoto 2008: 142).

2.3.5 Depictions/Painting on Vessels from the Yayoi Period

Some scholars have explored questions regarding social change during the Jōmon and Yayoi periods by analyzing pictorial expressions. As Kobayashi Seiji 小林青樹 (2007: 29) states, the concepts of patriarchy and war were absent in the Jōmon period, yet depictions of such scenes can be found on objects dated to the Yayoi period. Kobayashi explored a series of ritual scenes depicted on painted earthenware and bronze bells that show different tasks associated with men and women. Through examining the ceremonial scenes, he pointed out that on the right side of a temple a fertility rite is performed by a female priest dressed in bird's attire, followed on the left by a ritual of protection for the harvest performed by a male with a sword and shield. There is a clear distinction made between the men's and women's labor in both rice farming and rituals. That difference is displayed both spatially and temporally through representations of human and animal bodies in Yayoi imagery. Furthermore, it was suggested that the Yayoi period was a peaceful time with agricultural stability, although "wounded/damaged human bones" dated from the early Yayoi period in western Japan during the 1990s suggested that there were brutal wars during that time. Kobayashi suggested that wars not only led to a state of social tension but promoted patriarchy and the notion of female servitude under male rule. The social turmoil coincided with both the beginnings of rice farming and the wishes for a more stable and peaceful society. Furthermore, he suggested that ritual goods in Yayoi paintings were used as an instrument to adjust to such changing relationships (Kobayashi 2007: 28–29).

2.3.6 Mounded Tombs and Leadership in the Kofun Period

The Kofun period witnessed a great change in the sociopolitical system and male–female rulership, which manifested in mounded graves. Gina Barnes has put forth hypotheses on early Kofun rulership, ideology, and gender, based on material culture in elite burial customs of the Kofun period (Barnes 2012, 2014). In the discussion of the emergence of rulership and the state in early Japan, Barnes (2012) suggested the assemblage of burial goods in most early Kofun periods was associated with ritual purpose, while that of Middle Kofun, such as armor and weaponry, was more related to military purpose. That indicates the leadership was changed from "a ceremonial form of rulership to one based on military might" (Barnes 2012: 80). Barnes further argued that it was important to put early Japan into an East Asian context that emphasized the connections between Japan and the Chinese cultural tradition about Queen Mother mythology and the interactions between elite members of Yamato in Japan with those of Paekche on the Korean peninsula. Barnes indicated that the ritual burial system in the early Kofun period may be connected to the early Shinto practice in which female gods and female shamans played an important role politically. During the late fifth century, the Middle Kofun period appeared to have a stronger hierarchical structure in burials with more crafted artifacts and weaponry, which may be the result of interactions with the Korean peninsula (Barnes 2012: 87).

Supported by archaeological data, historical documents, and myths, Barnes (2007, 2012, 2014) provided a theory that the early Kofun rulers had adopted the myth and ideology of the Chinese Queen Mother of the West. The distribution of mounded tombs, stone chambers, jade objects, and bronze mirrors with the image of the Queen Mother suggests a strong connection with features of the Chinese Queen Mother. She further argued that Amaterasu, the Japanese Sun Goddess, was possibly "an extension of Queen Mother," reformed during the fifth to seventh centuries and later serving as the symbol of political legitimization for the imperial family of Japan (Barnes 2014).

Seike Akira 清家章, an archaeologist with a focus on kinship systems, gender, and social issues of the Kofun period, has actively excavated several burial mounds of the Kofun period. Examining the archaeological data from the Kofun tombs of both female and male leaders, Seike (2018) discerned that the Middle Kofun period was a transitional phase, from a female-and-male ruled society to a patrilineal society. Seike's study indicates that the Kofun period experienced a succession of chiefdoms and that female chieftains had ruled since the Yayoi but by the middle of the Kofun that custom had disappeared (Seike 2018: 233–234). Imai Takashi 今井堯, the first archaeologist to seriously analyze women's burial goods, points out that since women's funerary items included mirrors, bracelet-shaped stone items, weapons, and agricultural tools, in addition to ornaments, the female leaders must have been involved in rituals, military activity, and agricultural production (Imai 1982). Additionally, Seike suggests that it is highly possible that female chieftains had the same authority as male chiefs (Seike 2010, 2018: 226), and although it was highly possible that men and women both carried out rituals, leading rituals should be regarded as an authority peculiar to women (Yoshie 1996; Seike 2010, 2018).

It was war and the militarization of the regime that brought about sociopolitical change during the Middle Kofun period, according to Seike (2018). Archaeological evidence from the Kofun tombs suggests that female leaders were buried with swords and spears, and most of them were found outside of coffins. But there are very few cases in which knives were buried in the coffins of females; for example, in the early Kofun period, these knives are all less than 20 cm in length and thus cannot be used as swords or weapons but must have been utilitarian tools (Seike 2018: 226). On the other hand, in the coffins of males, swords of all sizes and lengths were deposited and the difference is obvious. In other words, in the burials of women in the early Kofun period, no weapons were placed in the coffin. The act of locating burial items outside the coffin did not occur from the beginning of the Yayoi but was common practice in the later Yayoi. This new custom may have been given a meaning that was not previously attached to funerary goods. Many researchers, such as Izumori Kō

泉森皎, have pointed out that swords located outside the coffin denote protection from evil spirits for the deceased (Izumori 1985). If the sword placed outside the coffin connoted protection/avoidance from evil, the knives in female tombs would not be considered a weapon. This trend is found consistently across all levels of society in male burials (Seike 2018: 226). In addition, the patrilineal kinship group within chiefdom hierarchies suggests that men were at the center of the ruling organization. The manner of succession of the chief from the middle period onwards does not contradict the succession of status revealed by Yoshie Akiko 義江明子 (Yoshie 1996) and has not changed to this day (Seike 2018: 234).

2.3.7 DNA Analysis from the Remains in Tombs of the Kofun Period

In recent years, DNA analysis has been beneficial for gendered archaeology. By using DNA analysis of human remains from the Kofun tombs at the Isoma Iwakage site (磯間岩陰遺跡) (ca. late fifth century to sixth century CE) in Wakayama Prefecture (和歌山県), Seike Akira (2021) studied how DNA analysis helps interpret the relationship between burial goods and human remains. For example, in chamber no. 1 a middle-aged man and a three-year-old boy were found. Although identification of children's biological sex was impossible to determine until very recently, with the help of DNA analysis these two have been proven to have had a second-degree of kinship. Thus, the blood relationship between the two is either grandfather and grandson or uncle and nephew. Prior to the DNA analysis, the author argued that the minor in this chamber was expected to inherit the position of the elder. This was thought to be confirmed because two swords with deer antler ornaments, Rokkaku-soken (鹿角装剣), were found in chamber no. 1: one sword with each body as burial goods. Seike suggested that it is possible that chamber no. 1 shows the beginning of the practice of hereditary succession of social positions among men, since the deer antler sword was given to the leader of the Isoma group. Thus, the three-year-old boy in this case could have been designated as the leadership successor because of the presence of the sword and the DNA finding. Additionally, in chamber no. 2, two adult women and one child were buried. All three shared the same mitochondria DNA, or were maternal relatives. Interestingly, none of them share the same mitochondria DNA with two bodies in chamber no. 1. More research needs to be completed to reflect accurately if there was a blood relationship between those buried in chambers no. 1 and no. 2.

Chamber no. 2 was constructed at the same time or slightly later than chamber no. 1 and contains the second largest number of grave goods after chamber no. 1. For Seike, this marks the beginning of hereditary social positions among men while at the same time showing that others were strongly tied through maternal lineage. This analysis supports previous research by Yoshiyuki Tanaka, who argued that after the end of the Middle Kofun period prioritization of paternal ties advanced, and until then both paternal and maternal ties were considered equally important. Since this is an ongoing project, Seike noted that the work of DNA analysis is continuing and there may still be many interesting topics related to gender, the history of women, and the history of kinship in the stone chambers no. 1 and no. 2. Seike also reminds researchers that we must be careful about when and when not to rupture human remains of collected samples as doing so does not guarantee that the remaining DNA will be in pristine condition (Seike 2021).

2.3.8 Meetings on Gender and Archaeology: Jōmon and Yayoi

It is worth noting that the first panel on gender archaeology in Japan was held on October 27, 2019, at the University of Okayama. The organizers, Matsumoto Naoko and Mitsumoto Jun, stated in their introduction that Japanese archaeology has been dominated by a cultural-historical approach. They emphasized the need for perspectives on gender to provide a new way to reexamine issues associated with social norms, behaviors, and worldviews since they have fundamentally changed in current times and society (Matsumoto and Mitsumoto 2022). Additionally, the five papers presented at the conference focused on four important issues: (1) childbirth, longevity, and kinship structure; (2) division of labor as gendered roles; (3) the reality of gender categories; and (4) the research environment for women. Summaries of the papers are available on the website and show a variety of methods and research questions posed by the group.[11]

Additionally, among these five papers, three of them have since been published in English in the *Japanese Journal of Archaeology* in March 2022. Igarashi Yuriko (2022) reported the latest research results on the patterns of fertility and survivorship among the Jōmon and Yayoi peoples by examining human skeletal remains from archaeological data, such as pregnancy parturition scars (PPS) on the ilium for fertility and age from the auricular surface for survivorship. The results suggested that the patterns of fertility and survivorship were different among the Jōmon and Yayoi populations. Additionally, Igarashi also compared the data from two Yayoi sites and found that different environments may determine the rates of fertility and survivorship – for example, a higher birth rate and greater longevity of women were found in the plains area than for women in the hill area (Igarashi 2022: 182–183). Igarashi

[11] The Japanese Archaeological Association, http://archaeology.jp/convention/2019okayama/.

suggested that further study is required to answer what caused these differences and whether they are because of differences in climate and regions or because of different time periods. Funahashi Kyōko's (2022) research studies how tooth extraction was associated with ritual activities and reflected the social organization from the Late Jōmon to Early Yayoi periods in western Japan. Funahashi examined how the different types of tooth extraction were associated with age and sex and suggested that ritual tooth extraction was associated with gender expressions and the sociocultural system. Mitsumoto Jun (2022) discussed the modalities of cross-dressing bodily representation in light of gendered roles for men and women in the Yayoi and Kofun periods. Mitsumoto suggested that cross-dressing related to the social structure of the time and that men's clothing was associated with social hierarchy during the Kofun period.

2.3.9 Summary and Hopes for Future Study

Inspired by Western feminist studies, current studies on gender in Japanese archaeology are mainly led by a few female scholars both inside and outside of Japan. They consider archaeological and visual evidence to reconstruct kinship and ritual systems through examination of depictions of gendered activities and the structure of leadership. Material remains in collections all across Japan can be used for further investigation of gendered roles in all early periods. Collaborative work with archaeologists from across Asia would, naturally, help break down barriers across national boundaries and allow for more inclusive and accurate reconstruction of ancient societies in northeast Asia.

As a plea for more gendered analysis, Fujimura (1998: 74) stated at the end of her article,

> Since it is an undeniable fact that women have lived and continued to work no less than men, I believe that as fellow women, we should never lose interest in women who lived in the ancient past. But we must keep in mind the objectivity that is necessary when we research; we should not be biased and should remind ourselves that we may find some facts that may not be directly connected to us living today. Many feminists have lost that objectivity and have been pushed to the margins of academia. Therefore, I sincerely hope that more and more colleagues will continue to ask simple questions calmly without being overwhelmed by the male-centered academic world.

Her encouraging words inspired many women scholars and hopefully will continue to reassure and persuade others to consider gender as a viable topic for study.

2.4 Mongolia

2.4.1 Historical Setting and Current Thinking

As in other areas of modern Asia, national identity has been an ever-present issue for archaeologists, anthropologists, historians, linguists, and art historians, among others, who are interested in Mongolia and most especially in the history of pastoralism. This lifeway has long been perceived as egalitarian and distinct from state-level societies with regard to societal complexity. But as current research is pointing out, pastoral societies do develop societal complexity, although its format may be different from that in state-level societies (Honeychurch 2014). Leadership roles and even everyday tasks for genders, for instance, may vary in pastoral communities depending on the time of year, needs of the herding activities across the seasons, specific tasks such as sheering vs. carding and weaving, and so on (Wright 2016). Thus, with its current welcoming attitude toward collaborative and scientific research, including the study of effects of climate and ecology on types of adaptation, Mongolia has become a lively place for research on pastoralism and including the roles of men and women in that system.

With a long history of an independent as well as a colonized territory, the modern nation both respects its history and has borrowed ideas, materials, and technology from its neighbors across time. The study of the origins of the Mongolian people and their heritage does occupy its local scholars, while the formation and dominance of empires located in its sovereign lands often have been the focus of research carried out by foreign investigators. Several features of its past and present have shaped the study of the peoples of present-day Mongolia.

With a population of just 3.3 million, Mongolia and much of its surrounding area is covered by grassy steppe, with mountains to the north and west and the Gobi Desert to the south. Ulaanbaatar, the capital and largest city, is home to roughly half of the country's population. The territory of modern-day Mongolia has been ruled by various nomadic empires, including the Xiongnu (匈奴), the Xianbei (鲜卑), the Rouran (柔然), the First Turkish Khaganate, and others. In 1206, Genghis Khan (Чингис хаан) founded the Mongol Empire, which became the largest contiguous land empire in history. Mongolia declared independence in 1911 after the fall of the Chinese monarchy and achieved actual separation in 1921. Shortly thereafter, the country became a satellite state of the Soviet Union in 1924. After the anti-communist revolutions of 1989, Mongolia conducted its own peaceful democratic revolution in 1990. This led to a new constitution in 1992.

This new independence has generated avenues of study and opened its territories to both indigenous and foreign collaborations. A Center for Gender Studies (жендэр судлалын төв) was founded in 2006 at the National University of Mongolia by Tsetsegjargal Tseden (Цэцэгжаргал Цэдэн; ᠴᠡᠴᠡᠭᠵᠠᠷᠭᠠᠯ ᠴᠡᠳᠡᠨ), who conducts research on contemporary Mongolian women. The study and analysis of gender issues in the early, ancient periods are a very recent focus there and fall into three research categories, each with a unique set of questions:

1. Historical studies making use of texts: primarily *The Secret History of the Mongols* (蒙古秘史, Монголчуудын нууц товчоо).
2. Archaeological investigation and reporting of men and women in burials and campsites.
3. Scientific studies of archaeological materials.

2.4.2 Historical Studies Making Use of Texts: Primarily The Secret History of the Mongols

Although the story of the Mongols has captivated the imagination of many historians since the rise of the Mongol Empire in the twelfth century CE, the oldest extant text, *The Secret History of the Mongols* (蒙古秘史; Монголчуудын нууц товчоо), was probably written down soon after Genghis Khan's death in the mid thirteenth century in a script borrowed from the Uighur Turks. Based on oral traditions, it is the official history of the literate royal family. Our source today is a Chinese manuscript, copied in the Ming (明) dynasty after the Mongols were driven out of China (Atwood 2023). Its perceptions were based both on myth and actual behavior, but that text is the only premodern written document we have from a purportedly Mongol point of view (Greaves 2020; Broadbridge 2018) and it clearly persists today among Mongolian women and often historians (Avery 2000; Rossabi n.d.), and it may also offer clues or cautions for interpretating gender roles in the past.

The roles of women in the *Secret History* have been pointed out by Anne Broadridge (2018) and Aspen Greaves (2020). They identified female "types" described and recorded as great and lesser mothers, revealing a hierarchy among women; political actors gained through their husbands' and/or their own lineage; hostages or women captured and taken as wives; and domineering rulers who acted as regents three notable times (Greaves 2020: 8–25). They note that these royal women affected the lives of their families first and foremost, but when thrust into political roles they were also effective managers and leaders. Should such evidence of royal life be found archaeologically, these roles might be reflected in evidence of marriage, of accumulation of wealth, weapons, and elaborate embellishments, in tributes from children, and so on.

A recent study of the emergence of empire in Eurasia and its effects on contiguous polities posits that these pastoral peoples were responsible for significant innovations in governing, among others, the Xiongnu in Mongolia (Beckwith 2023). Beckwith called these peoples Scythians and dated their existence from as early as the ninth century BCE in Tuva and western Mongolia. His arguments depend almost wholly on Greek and Chinese texts, and he largely ignores archaeological evidence. He does recount stories of male leaders and female warriors.

2.4.3 Excavated Contexts and the Treatment of Gender

In a recent excavation (2020) of a cemetery at the Airagiin Gozgor archaeological site (Айрагийн гозгор), located in the Orkhon province (Орхон) of northern Mongolia, twenty-nine burials were discovered by researchers from the California State University – Los Angeles. Professors Christine Lee and Yahaira Gonzalez led the excavations and found evidence of three groups buried there: the Xiongnu, who dominated the region 2,200 years ago; the Xianbei, who overtook the Xiongnu around 1,850 years ago; and the Turkic people, who successively occupied the Mongolian prairies around 1,470 years ago (Cascone 2020).

Such excavations have suggested combat military roles for women. After examination of human remains, Lee discovered significant markings on three female Xiongnu skeletons that suggest they may have occasionally practiced archery or horseback riding, while the Turkic skeletons only did horseback riding. But two female skeletons out of three at the Xianbei burial (147–552 CE) stood out as riders and possibly skilled fighters (Cascone 2020; Gegel 2020).

In a cogent essay on household archaeology of mobile pastoralists informed by survey data from Egiin Gol, Josh Wright used archaeological results and ethnographic research in the same areas to look at how gender figured in the spatial use of the sites (Wright 2016: 143–144). He argued that with the aid of scientific methods of analysis ranging from geomorphology to molecular archaeology he could suggest how space was used daily and seasonally for these mobile people.

To do so, he used:

1. Ceramic distributions to give information on high-traffic areas and activities in general.

2. Faunal studies to provide information on foddering and penning practices.
3. Soil and soil chemistry studies.

He found that women were most active in or near the *ger* (гэр), in the kitchen, at hitching lines, and at animal standing areas or corrals, whereas men were likely most active along animal paths into and out of the campsite and in open areas where animals were divided by sex and age. The exchange of animals and duties between genders occurred as well. Women and female animals were most active in the spaces within a campsite, while lone men and mixed animal groups were most active in the broader landscape.

These two studies show that men and women had defined roles in society, that there was a hierarchy within genders, and that a clear ordering of the space was followed by the family. Local functioning of the household was carried out by women while external activity was men's work. A special category for women existed in some pastoral communities that provided military assistance when needed (Cascone 2020; Gegel 2020). This would not necessarily have been a full-time, year-round role for either men or women (Linduff and Rubinson 2022: 82–88), but the studies on human bones at least confirm that some women were mounted warriors. An even more recent volume gives another point of view (see below, Miller 2024)

2.4.4 Scientific Studies of Archaeological Materials

In addition to the studies by Gegel (2000) and Cascone (2000), both informed by scientific analyses of archaeological remains, the rise in interest in human biological remains in ancient pastoral communities as evidenced in Mongolia is significant. Proceeding from a point of caution, Crawford warns that mobile pastoralists developed different patterns of social organization that depended on their specific ecological, cultural, political, or historical circumstances. Each geographical region had its own unique pattern of development and interaction with the surrounding sedentary societies, and the genetic and demographic structure of pastoral populations was shaped by aspects of their distinctive subsistence ecology (Crawford and Leonard 2002: 8). Studies that provide information about sex and age, health, diet, family structure, family and genetic affiliation, conflict and trauma, and activity-related morphologies have been conducted (among others, e.g., Holliman 2011; Murphy et al. 2013; Erdene 2013; Eng 2013, 2015; Eng and Zhang 2013; Keyser et al. 2020). Taken together, such studies can merge the ecological, demographic, health, and biological facets of the herding existence and often get at defining roles for each sex. The recent synthetic study on the Xiongnu by Bryan Miller will hopefully lead to further research and interpretation on gendered behaviors (Miller 2024).

Making use of other types of testing, for instance, Keyser et al. (2020) have generated nuclear and whole mitochondrial DNA data from the skeletal remains of fifty-two individuals excavated from the Tamir Ulaan Khoshuu cemetery (Тамир Улаан Хошуу) in Central Mongolia used by the Xiongnu from the first century BCE to the first century CE. Kinship analyses were conducted using autosomal and Y-chromosomal DNA markers along with complete sequences of the mitochondrial genome in order to conduct genetic studies of family, parity, and conquest in Iron Age Xiongnu. These analyses suggested close kin relationships between many individuals and that nineteen such individuals comprised a large family spanning five generations. Within this family, they determined that one woman was of especially high status, offering a novel insight into the structure and hierarchy of societies from the Xiongnu period. Moreover, they confirmed that, in the group studied, the Xiongnu had a strongly admixed mitochondrial and Y-chromosome gene pool and a significant western component. Using a fine-scale approach (haplotype instead of haplogroup-level information), they proposed that Scytho-Siberians were ancestors of the Xiongnu and Huns their descendants. Although results are always up for review, this is the sort of detailed and insightful research underway.

An important new study of Xiongnu genomic structures among populations on the western frontier of the empire in western Mongolia has found very clear indications of gendered status and roles in the local sites studied. While the high-status tombs are largely female and are of eastern Eurasian ancestry, the secondary tombs adjacent are of males of western Eurasian ancestry, for instance. In addition, several female tombs also showed a concentration of wealth and elite status that included exotic items from further east, such as Chinese silks, lacquers, and so on, suggesting that interregional connections to groups in Han Dynasty China may have been greater, and more complex, than previously understood. This also suggests that Xiongnu women played an especially prominent role in the expansion and integration of new territories along the empire's frontier (Lee et al. 2023). This new study confirms with certainty the flexible status of females and males in Xiongnu society that had been suggested earlier, but in a study based only on archaeological materials (Linduff 2008: 181–191; Miller 2024).

2.4.5 Now and in the Future

Although gender studies are still in their infancy in Mongolia, research is welcomed on gender issues and materials have been made available to scientists for the most recent types of testing. More surveys and excavations are being conducted and international collaboration is welcomed, so deeper knowledge of the lifeways of the various peoples of Mongolia and their interaction with others will undoubtedly be forthcoming. And, as women form an important part of the archaeology roster at National University of Mongolia, and given that gender issues are an important part of the history of pastoral peoples, more and more sophisticated studies will likely appear.

2.5 Taiwan

2.5.1 Historical Setting and Gender Ideology in Taiwan

The current and historical geopolitical situation in Taiwan has created a very particular setting regarding the study of gender and many other topics. Located in East Asia in the northwestern Pacific Ocean, Taiwan is situated in a strategic region with a complex history of waves of migration and changing regimes, especially during the twentieth century due to the rapid political changes in East Asia. Since the early Neolithic period, migrants from the south and southeast coasts of the mainland arrived in Taiwan, leading some to suggest that the east coast of Taiwan was a homeland for ancient Austronesian people (Tsang 2005a). During the Ming and Qing dynasties, more and more Han Chinese came to Taiwan from China's southeast coast. Around the first half of the seventeenth century, Dutch and Spanish colonists occupied Taiwan briefly. After the Sino-Japanese War in 1895, Taiwan was ceded to Japan by the Qing government and became a colony of Japan. In 1945, Taiwan was returned to China under the government of the Republic of China after World War II. After four years of civil war in China, the Nationalist Party of China (referred to as the Kuomintang, or KMT) retreated to Taiwan in 1949, while Martial Law (May 20, 1949 to July 14, 1987) was issued and was not lifted until July 15, 1987 as proclaimed by President Chiang Ching-kuo 蔣經國 (1910–1988). Lee Teng-hui 李登輝 (1923–2020) succeeded as president in 1988 and was then elected as the president of the Republic of China. This initial process of democratization in Taiwan witnessed different social and political movements during the late 1980s and 1990s, including a feminist movement.

During Lee's time, political reconstruction was initiated, and a debate on Taiwan's national identity among its intellectuals was raised beginning in the early 1990s (Jiang 1998). Additionally, in 1997, textbooks were revised to reconstruct Taiwanese identity with more moderate ideas and to emphasize multiculturalism (Wang 2000). President Lee Teng-hui openly defined the special relationship between China and Taiwan as "two states" in 1999 (Sheng 2002). Such changes in the political environment inside and outside of

Taiwan have caused a change in how people in Taiwan, including in terms of gender, identify themselves. For example, during the late 1990s the dominant Chinese nationalist ideal was replaced by a dual national identity (both Chinese and Taiwanese), and from 2001 to 2019 more people formed yet another Taiwanese national identity (Shen 2022: 73–93). Beginning in the early 1990s, recognition that Taiwan had hosted several different cultural and ethnic groups in the past has led to making a multicultural history the basis of a newly formed national identity.

In that environment, the study of gender in Taiwan was influenced by the feminist movement in the West from the 1980s. A center for gender studies was founded in 1985 with the support of the Asia Society, which was placed under the Center for Population of the National Taiwan University. The first journal on gender studies was published in 1990 and the center established the first Women and Gender Studies program in 1997, which has focused on women's roles and gender studies on contemporary Taiwanese women.[12] Furthermore, like many Western countries, a same-sex marriage bill was passed by the Taiwanese parliament with the support of the Democratic Progressive Party (DPP) on May 24, 2019, and made Taiwan the first country in Asia to allow same-sex couples to register their relationships. The implementation of this law helped engender marriage equality (Friedman and Chen 2023) and marked Taiwan's search for new models, including a gendered ideology.

Currently, Taiwan's sociopolitical environment, democratization, and the women's movement have made it one of the most gender-friendly countries in Asia, according to Chen Yi-chien (2021). Scholars have studied the lives of women and men in modern and contemporary Taiwan from historical, sociopolitical, and cross-cultural perspectives (Farris et al. 2004). Lu Hsin-yi (2004) examined the origins of Taiwanese feminist thought during Japanese rule (1895–1945) and argued that feminism arose partially out of the gendered rhetoric in Taiwanese intellectual discussion, which was regarded as a signifier of modernity during the 1920s and 1930s. Catherine Farris (2004) provided a comprehensive and thoughtful comparative study on women in China and Taiwan. Farris compared the influences of socialist developments in China and capitalist expansion in Taiwan on the lives of women and examined several aspects of women's lives from the late Qing dynasty to the 1990s.

Although scholarship in gender studies has focused on modern and contemporary society, gender studies of ancient society have only begun in recent years. Importantly, with the efforts by the current government to present itself as

[12] Information about the history of the Women's and Gender Research program is available on the Center's website: https://gender.psc.ntu.edu.tw/small-histroy/ (accessed October 5, 2023).

a separate and distinct nation independent from the PRC, they have seemingly affected the direction of studies of ancient Taiwan to include the multicultural background of the island population. This allows for study of distinctive gender roles as exhibited in the varied cultures that inhabit the island even today.

2.5.2 Taiwan Archaeology and Ethnoarchaeology

Over the past five decades, the data from archaeological discoveries in Taiwan have enriched our understanding of the history of prehistoric and early historic periods, cultural exchanges and interactions between Taiwan and its neighboring territories, and the resulting development of social organization (Tsang 1995; Liu 2019; Pearson 2023). Since the early Neolithic period, migrants from the south and southeast coasts of the mainland arrived in Taiwan, and archaeological data show that Tapenkeng 大坌坑 pottery with cord-marked rim and neck, for instance, was associated with the Pearl River Delta (Tsang 2005b: 71). Recognizing the many sources of Taiwanese culture, Liu Yi-chang 劉益昌 (2006) addressed the issue of construction of national and regional history through the study of Taiwan's prehistoric and early historical periods to include Indigenous groups. But as Chiang Chih-hua 江芝華 has pointed out, the discourse on Taiwan's prehistoric period still mainly focuses on objects, such as the study of remains, dates, living conditions, transportation, and exchange systems (Chiang 2008: 126), and the study of gender from an archaeological perspective is very limited. On the other hand, Chen Po-chan's 陈伯桢 review of Taiwan's ethnoarchaeology suggests that ethnographic and anthropological research in Taiwan provides an alternative way to study ancient societies through the inclusion of Indigenous groups of people in Taiwan (Chen 2009). Since the social systems of Indigenous groups in Taiwan are different from traditional Chinese society, scholars have studied the construction of gender identity and gender roles in their societies separately.

2.5.3 Archaeology and Scientific Testing of Human Bones

Some analyses using scientific testing have yielded interesting results about gender and age. A group of archaeologists have also examined dental conditions and human skeletons from two archaeological sites in Taiwan and observed changes in food consumption and health conditions from the earliest Neolithic period (3000 BCE) to the later Iron Age (200–1500 CE) (Pietrusewsky et al. 2013). The human skeletons are from two archaeological sites: twenty-three individuals are from the Nankuanli East (南關裡東) (NKLE) site located in the Tainan Science Park (台南科學院區), Tainan City, which belongs to the Tapenkeng culture (ca. 5000 years BP [ca. 3000

BCE]). The second group from the Iron Age Shisanhang site (十三行) (SSH) (ca. 1800–500 years BP [ca. 200–1500 CE]) located in northwestern Taiwan also has twenty-three individuals. The data from the Tapenkeng Neolithic site shows overall that the dental health of the individuals from the NKLE was good, but the frequency of advanced wearing away of the teeth was significantly higher in adult males than in adult women, which might be related to age, diet, and/or lifestyle. The data from the SSH site suggest that children's health had improved over time. During the Iron Age, because more soft foods were provided, tooth wear was reduced. The inhabitants of both sites engaged in agriculture, fishing, and exploitation of marine and terrestrial resources. The data show that early Neolithic residents in Taiwan were under greater physiological stress than residents of Iron Age sites. Overall, Taiwan's prehistoric residents had good dental health. This also appeared to reflect a nonagricultural economy and probably the consumption of marine foods that were low in starch, sugar, and/or caries deficiencies (Pietrusewsky et al. 2013).

The remains of tooth ablation rituals in Taiwan have been found from Neolithic and Iron Age sites, traced back to 2500 BCE, and were a unique rite of passage for women (Chiu 2010). Chiu Hung-lin 邱鴻霖 studied the tooth ablation ritual based on ethnographies with reference to 162 skeletons found in the burials from the Neolithic Shih-chiao site (石橋遺址), Tainan County (台南), Taiwan (Niaosung culture 蔦松文化, 1200–1700 BP [800–300 CE]) (Chiu 2010). Among the 162 skeletons, 59 had tooth ablations. More importantly, the tooth ablation ritual, both maxillary lateral incisor and canine teeth ablated symmetrically, was performed mainly on teenage and young adult females, although no evidence showed a connection between pregnancy and tooth ablation. At the same time, it was not associated with particular natal groups since the analysis of tooth crowns showed that some individuals were genetically connected and some were not. Chiu suggested that tooth ablation was highly correlated with adulthood and marital status.

2.5.4 Gender and Social Order: Archaeology of "House Societies"

Chiang adopted the concept of "House Societies" proposed by Lévi-Strauss in the 1950s and suggested that this concept offers archaeologists a useful approach to examining the social organization and material culture of Taiwan's prehistoric period (Chiang 2008). Chen Yu-pei 陳有貝 (2015) examined the distribution of the ornaments and changes in their function and symbolic meanings found in prehistoric sites in Taiwan across space and time. For example, during the Neolithic period the use of ornaments varied by region and culture, while during the Iron Age there was a new development in production and use associated with social change.

Two studies on aboriginal groups are related to gender and the use of house space. Based on Chiang Bien 蔣斌 and Li Ching-yi's 李靜怡 ethnographic study of the Paiwan group (排灣族) (Chiang and Li 1995), the family house of the Paiwan people has extremely rich connotations in relation to social life and cosmology. Family houses were inherited by the couple's eldest heir, either male or female. The eldest heir who inherits the house and family business is called *vusam*, meaning millet seed, in Paiwanese. This suggests that the eldest heir is synonymous with millet seeds and according to Paiwan beliefs is used as a seed storage while the younger siblings are equated with sown millet endlessly spread to multiply the original family numbers. Moreover, the Paiwan people practice indoor burial. In addition to the dormitory, fire pit, storage room, stone niche altar on the back wall, and other facilities, the burial pit is located within a living space, one of the most sacred interior spaces of a family house where the sculptures of ancestors in pillar format were set into the corners. Paiwan couples are not buried in the same tomb after death, because husband and wife were not born in the same house. Brothers and sisters at the age of marriage leave home to marry but return to their hometown to be buried. The structure, internal space facilities, inheritance, and naming of the family house and their dependence on ancestral spirits are closely related to the social identity and status of Paiwan people from birth to death (Chiang and Li 1995). Furthermore, Kuo Su-chiu 郭素秋 suggested that the gender-neutral relationship between the original house and its subdivisions signifies "the reproduction of Paiwan society" and was embodied in ideas about millet and family groupings (Kuo 2023: 190–191).

2.5.5 The Austronesian Identifiers: Food and Burial Factors

By studying a complex of culture groups, Taiwan archaeology has documented diversity of food production, material remains, and cultural activities. It has been suggested that Taiwan's Neolithic marks the first stage in the expansion of Austronesian-speaking people, from its southeastern coastal China origins through the Pacific (Hung and Carson 2014). The discussion is about how the origins of the Taiwan Neolithic food production provided a context to understand how ancient Austronesian-speaking populations supplied themselves in Taiwan and ultimately settled throughout the Pacific. For example, archaeobotanical findings suggest that Taiwan's Neolithic supported a broad range of food production, including tuber cultivation, farming, fishing, and foraging. These were all crucial components of a Neolithic package, though rice and millet cultivation ultimately became important as well. As the authors suggested, food availability and production were one of the great motivations that made early peoples migrate, and foragers and fishers might have been great explorers who moved from coastal China to Taiwan and then from Taiwan to the Pacific islands (Hung and Carson 2014: 1129). Food production may have become a cultural memory later fabricated into the myth of origin, for example, of the goddess of Kavalan (噶瑪蘭), one of the aboriginal groups in Taiwan. We will discuss this as reviewed by Liu Pi-chen 劉璧榛 (2007, 2008, 2020).

Other cultural features proposed to connect Taiwan and the Pacific islands are based on new archaeological evidence. Based on the study of burial jars and burial practice, Tsang Cheng-hwa 臧振華 has suggested that it was possible that the east coast of Taiwan was a homeland for ancient people of both Lanyu (蘭嶼), an island located about 90 km southeast of Taitung (台東), and Batanes Islands (巴丹島), islands located 162 km north of Luzon, in the Philippines, although some of the Yami (雅美) legends of Lanyu indicate that their ancestors came from the islands of Batanes. According to archaeological data from recent excavations at the Huanggangshan site (黃岡山遺址) in Hualian County (花蓮縣) and the Wanshan site (丸山遺址) in Yilan County (宜蘭縣), Tsang suggested that the forms and practices of these jar burials are similar to those found on Lanyu and Batanes, but their dates were earlier, suggesting that the jar burial tradition on both Lanyu and Batanes may ultimately have originated in Taiwan (Tsang 2005a).

2.5.6 Gender in Belief Systems

In her studies of the goddesses of aboriginal groups in Taiwan, Liu Pi-chen 劉璧榛 (2007, 2008, 2020) has researched beliefs, especially in the *mutumazu* goddess, in relation to the matrilineal and matrilocal social structure (only partially retained in later ruling systems) of the Kavalan people (噶瑪蘭) in Taiwan. It is believed that the *matumazu* goddess brought rice plants to their land and was the mother of *mtiu*, female shamans (Liu 2007: 48–50). Liu Pi-chen's ethnographical studies have enriched our understanding about the complicated relationship between gender construction, religious symbolic representation, and food in aboriginal societies (Liu 2007). In Kavalan matrilineal society, women have their own ritual groups, fields, and gender symbols. The relationship between women and food (rice goddess) is established via matrilineal inheritance. Women acquire power within the scope of religion, family, and related material control, as well as their power to communicate with the supernatural. In contrast, males are associated with wild deer and must achieve social status through ability, tools, and the total amount of prey and types of prey they accumulate. But men and women also establish interdependent connections because of these social differences. Liu also suggested that gender construction and food production, consumption as well as exchange, are established through continuous interaction and are not instituted or unchanged categories (Liu 2007: 62).

In contrast, the Goddess Mazu (媽祖) was associated with the Han Chinese who immigrated from the mainland. Chang Hsun 張珣 studied the Mazu cult within an anthropological study of goddess worship and suggested that Matsu was a virgin, an unmarried woman, was called a spirited woman in the early period, but was identified as a Heavenly Queen, or Saint Mother, indicating that she had been identified as an ideal Chinese woman (Chang 1995: 199). If all of these concepts had archaeological correlates, and they are likely to have, they are yet to be discovered.

2.5.7 First Journal Articles on Gender Archaeology

The first journal article focused on gender studies in archaeology was published in April 2020, edited by Chiang Chih-hua 江芝華, an associate professor in the Department of Anthropology at National Taiwan University and a research fellow in the Women's Studies program under the Center for Population of the National Taiwan University. As Chiang Chih-hua has pointed out, gender archaeology has been discussed in the West since the 1980s, but as a subfield it has not been taken seriously in Taiwanese archaeological discourse. Yet, in the twenty-first century and with the growing number of women archaeologists and the rise in diversity in the Taiwanese archaeological community, discussions on gender and the archaeological methods used to discern it began to increase, leading to a volume focused on how female scholars/archaeologists study gender in ancient societies (Chiang 2020: 7). The following discussion reviews five articles from the journal, namely two on Taiwan, two on China, and one on Japan. These articles were not all focused on Taiwan, yet the area studies, including China, Japan, and Taiwan, may indicate Taiwan's diversity, historical past and present, and/or intellectual interests.

Ko Yu-chieh 柯渝婕 (2020) focused on the 4,451 ceramic rings found in 23 pits at the Niaosung site (蔦松遺址), dated from around 1800–1400 BP or 200–600 CE. Ko proposed that it is important to put these rings into a cultural context since they had not been studied thoroughly and often were identified merely as ornaments. Based on the inner diameter of the ring, ranging from 3 cm to 20 cm, Ko suggested that both children and adults could have worn them (Ko 2020: 38). Since the shapes of pottery rings were within a certain range, from round to square with few changes over time, she suggested that it is possible that wearing pottery rings was a special meaning standardized for people at Niaosung. Although there were not enough data to analyze the precise social significance of wearing pottery rings, they were not particularly related to women. There must have been an acknowledgment within Niaosung society that wearing pottery rings was not based on gender, age, kinship, or class. Consequently, generations of people there wore them, a meaningful gesture not yet understood (Ko 2020: 38–39).

Chung Kuo-feng 鐘國風 (2020) examined both men and women's roles in Amis (阿美) adult ceremonies at Lidaw (裡漏部落), Dongchang Village (東昌村) in Hualian County (花蓮縣), but with particular attention paid to adult ceremonies for women, which had not been discussed previously. Among the aboriginal groups in Taiwan, the Amis are often seen as representatives of a matrilineal society. Bawsa (女子送飯給男子), a ritual that is embedded in the men's Boat Ritual ceremony (Palunan [船祭]), shows a teenage girl dressed in formal, traditional costume bringing food to a teenage boy. While those two ate together in a temporary space, during the ritual ceremony they were married and became adults. Subsequently, the woman who runs the house would receive help from her mother to buy a set of sacrificial clay pots, a ritual that reiterated the connection between home and ancestral spirits. Chung suggested that through the Amis Boat Ritual and Bawsa ritual, adolescents were transformed into adult men and women with gendered roles while at the same time it reinforced traditional Amis lifeways and a gender system in a matriarchal society (Chung 2020: 28–29).

Two other articles focused on China were written by two female scholars from the Institute of History and Philology at the Academia Sinica. Uchida Junko内田純子, a Japanese scholar born in Tokyo and trained in Chinese archaeology at Kyoto University, studied how gendered society formed as part of the process of urbanization during the Yinxu period by analyzing jade and bronze artifacts unearthed at the Yinxu (殷墟) site. She suggested that, after becoming urbanized, men had more time to develop professional skills such as learning how to write, making pottery or casting bronze, while women were limited to childbirth and nursing (Uchida 2020: 18–19). Lin Kuei-chen 林圭偵 (2020) discussed women in frontier areas, in Sichuan (四川). Lin connected her personal fieldwork experience in Sichuan areas and talked about the unconventional character of Sichuan's "spicy women" such as Bao Sanniang 鮑三娘, who was famous for the conquest of Nanman (南蠻). Additionally, Lin also introduced Zeng Zhaoyu 曾昭燏, China's first female archaeologist, who was trained at the University of London and was a classmate of Xia Nai 夏鼐, one of the founders of Chinese archaeology. Zeng Zhaoyu used scientific archaeological methods in Yunnan and built on studies of ethnic groups and cultures of the southwestern frontier.

Lu Jou-chun 盧柔君 (2020) discussed the changes and limitations in gender studies in Japanese archaeology and suggested that researchers should be more cautious not to use today's social structure and gender stereotypes to explain what happened in the past. Lu also mentioned that the reproductions of the ancient family in Taiwan's museums should pay attention to the stereotypes of gendered roles in ancient societies.

2.5.8 Museum Exhibitions and Gender

Museum exhibitions play an important role in educational purposes and the pursuit of historical knowledge, and since the early 1990s the material remains of Indigenous groups in Taiwan have been exhibited in the museums, including the Shung Ye Formosan Aborigines Museum, the National Museum of Prehistory. More importantly, the cultural diversity of Indigenous groups has been celebrated and presented as a part of Taiwan history and cultural traditions (Varutti 2011). For example, the exhibition on "Gender, Space, and Society of the Amis," curated by Chen Wende at the Museum of Ethnology of the Academia Sinica, shows how Amis men and women lived. Additionally, the representation of the members of a family from the Shihsanhang Museum of Archaeology in Taiwan projects a modern concept of a nuclear and idealized family – the parent with a boy and a girl. Even so, the range of topics on the archaeological study of gender in Taiwan has exhibited a view of history that acknowledges the contributions of many groups who came to Taiwan: aborigines, mainlanders from different culture areas, and Japanese. Recognition of the differences in the cultural practices of such groups, including gendered roles, could lead to an understanding of a more diverse society from the very beginning of the occupation of Taiwan. Certainly, affected by the desire to create a new national identity and to establish a distinctive pattern from that of the PRC, Taiwan archaeologists may formulate a more diverse picture of the past that does not seek Chinese identity but Taiwan's multiple identities that are unique to the island.

2.5.9 Future Considerations

Similar to Korean archaeology, many questions in Taiwanese archaeology are still needed to bring about careful and thoughtful interpretation, including those about gender. If incorporated into theoretical modeling, for instance, household archaeological investigations could include more scientific testing of human remains for sex identification, for gender-specific issues of diet, health, movement of peoples, division of labor, kinship and other social structures, and state development and ideology. Scientific know-how is clearly available in Taiwan's labs and its more extensive use will lead to more nuanced and sophisticated interpretations of gender in Taiwan. As in any study, the use of scientifically rendered data is most useful when set into the historical context.

3 Thinking Ahead

What this Element has made clear is the need for several types of rethinking about the paradigms currently applied in the scholarship. For example, as the example of Taiwan has shown, albeit perhaps unintentionally and under the guise of nationalistic objectives, all over East Asia identities are hybrid and pluralistic and there are more representative ways to think about ancient groupings of peoples than the traditional culture-historical paradigms so engrained in thinking about Asia. An abandonment of a cultural-historical approach to archaeological and binary interpretations based on an us/them mentality fueled by modern nationalist agendas would lead to other modes of interpretation (such as postcolonial and postmodern) and approaches to ethnicity, gender, and cultural identity, including hybridity, identity fluidity, and pluralistic conceptions showing that groups/peoples were not monolithic cultural blocks existing in opposition to each other but were intrinsically intertwined in communities sustained by adaptive approaches to social and cultural self-presentation.

Alternate groupings might include, among others, depending on the time period:

1. Coastal East Asia (Russian Far East, Taiwan, central coastal China, Philippines, Vietnam, Kyushu and the southern islands of Japan) (see Nelson 2013).
2. Northern Asia (Mongolia, northern Japan, Korea, northeastern China, Russian Far East) and Inner Asia.
3. Central China and Eurasia.

Within each, cultural hybridity was typical and discernable, but so was self-identification with non-colonial traditions vs. colonial expressions of dominance and power in frontier areas (e.g., Maoqinggou) or mixed expressions of affiliation even in the capital city (e.g., the tomb of the Shang royal consort Fu Hao 妇好墓).

Since binary concepts of identity fail to account for the nuances within the mixed communities of the regions, attempts to define what is meant by "gender" (or ethnicity, for that matter) as a sociological, anthropological, and archaeological category would be more productive. A thorough evaluation of a range of scholarly approaches, from the traditional (gender and ethnicity as related to common ancestry) to the postmodern (gender as a malleable tool for one's own self-representation), would lead to a much-needed attempt to bridge the traditions of Western and Eastern Asian scholarship, for example in marriage contracts and gender-based burial patterns.

Attempts to tackle other questions about identity would be fruitful as well. Are pluralistic identities created at a local level to mediate (colonializing of frontiers?, etc.) interactions that were shaped, but not supplanted, by the influence of colonialists' dominating ideas to conquer, integrate, make the subjugated "Chinese," "Japanese," and so on? That is, does the expanding culture push the local into new identity formation? If not, what other factors could be brought to bear?

The search for archaeological information on gender in early East Asia can be fruitful if pursued in relation to a conceptualization of gender following successful gender social theory in other parts of the world. An understanding of gender as a socially constructed concept, and one that is tied to the construction of multiple and fluid identities as affected by age, social status, occupation, state-level policies, ethnicity, historical circumstances, and many others, would give a fuller picture of how such positions affected community structures. Ethnographic parallels might inspire rethinking of such matters in an archaeological setting.

Research involving the use of excavated texts, archaeological materials, and scientific reasoning and testing would most likely require collaborative teams and result in more synthetic interpretations. More robust collection of data on historical contexts in which ideas about gender operated, and concentration on local studies, might lead to regional analyses that would more clearly represent ancient culture areas that cross current national boundaries.

Moreover, the inclusion of several of the following features in constructing research questions would surely target new understandings of gender: Family and class issues especially in relation to local behaviors in institutions such as marriage continue to be rewarding topics when examining regional alliances, class mobility, economic priorities, and so on. Consideration of flexible societal organization in local settings, including evidence of hierarchies and/or hierarchies even in the same locales, could lead to a deeper understanding of changing expectations for members of each gender. More focus on health conditions, including diet and its role in defining and marking genders and societal rank as aided by stable isotope and other types of testing and analysis of bone and teeth, would add further depth to understanding individual roles of members of the tested societies. Attention to familial relations, aided by DNA testing, when considering marriage customs, economic exchanges, military and economic strategies, and more, could make clearer the role of gender in decision-making about political, trade, and many other alliances. Awareness of housing and overall site organization that exposes evidence about family organization across gender, age, and class can reveal patterns that governed local and regional economies, community and individual work habits, funerary practices according to cultural affiliations, age, class, and gender, for instance, and may reveal gendered behavior within the family structure. Age testing when examining gendered roles in familial, social, and political arenas, as well as certain ritual ceremonies, can also be fruitful.

As many publications are either dissertations or conference papers published as edited volumes, it would be refreshing to have single-authored monographs in which an author could present an argument comprehensively. This would need to be built on case studies that concern the self-representation of individuals in their local context. Searches for resonance between differing disciplinary approaches among researchers in any such endeavor might lead to comparative as well as shared multi-vector analyses rather than the reporting of individual findings only in isolated, narrowly targeted venues.

Clearly the study of gender and ancient societies is on the minds of many scholars in East Asia, and hopefully this Element will aid them when considering new projects.

Bibliography

Akazawa Takeru 赤澤威, Minoru Yoneda 米田譲, and Yoshida Kunio 吉田邦夫 (1993). 北村縄文人骨の同位体食性分析 (Isotope Analysis on Diet from Human Bones at the Jomon Kitamura Site). In長野県埋蔵文化財センター (編) (Nagano Prefectural Centre for Buried Cultural Properties, eds.), 中央自動車道長野線 埋蔵文化財発掘調査報告書 11 明科町内-北村遺跡 (*Kitamura Site: Report 11 on the Excavations prior to the Nagano Prefecture Chuo Expressway Construction: Sites within Akashina-Town*). 名古屋: 日本道路公団名古屋建設局 (Nagoya: Nihon Dōro Kōdan Nagoya Kensetsukyoku), pp. 445–468.

Allard, F., Sun, Y., and Linduff, K. M., eds. (2018). *Memory and Agency in Ancient China*. Cambridge: Cambridge University Press.

Ames, K. M. (1995). Chiefly Power and Household Production on the Northwest Coast. In T. D. Price and G. M. Feinman, eds., *Foundations of Social Inequality*. New York: Plenum Press, pp. 155–187.

(2007). The Archaeology of Rank. In R. A. Bentley, H. D. G. Maschner, and C. Chippendale, eds., *Handbook of Archaeological Theories*. Lanham, MD: AltaMira Press, pp. 487–513.

Argawal, S. C. and Glencross, B. A. (2011a). *Social Bioarchaeology*. Malden, MA: Wiley-Blackwell.

(2011b). Building a Social Bioarchaeology. In S. C. Argawal and B. A. Glencross, eds., *Social Bioarchaeology*. Malden, MA: Wiley-Blackwell, pp. 1–11.

Atwood, C. P., trans. (2023). *The Secret History of the Mongols*. Penguin Classics. New York: Penguin Random House.

Avery, M. (2000). *Women of Mongolia*, 2nd ed. Seattle: University of Washington Press and Asian Art and Archaeology.

Bacus, E. A. (2006). Gender in East Asian and Southeast Asian Archaeology. In S. M. Nelson, ed., *Handbook of Gender in Archaeology*. Lanham, MD: AltaMira Press, pp. 667–690.

Barnes, G. L. (2006). *Women in the Nihon Shoki*: *Mates*, *Mothers*, *Mystics*, *Militarists*, *Maids*, *Manufacturers*, *Monarchs*, *Messengers and Managers*. Durham: Durham University Department of East Asian Studies.

(2007). *State Formation in Japan: Emergence of a 4th-Century Ruling Elite*. London: Routledge.

(2012). The Emergence of Political Rulership and the State in Early Japan. In K. F. Friday, ed., *Japan Emerging: Premodern History to 1850*. London: Routledge Press, pp. 77–88.

(2014). A Hypothesis for Early Kofun Rulership. *Japan Review*, 27(27), 3–29.

(2015). *Archaeology of East Asia: The Rise of Civilization in China, Korea, and Japan*. Oxford: Oxbow Books.

Barnes, G. L. and M. Hudson (1991). Yoshinogari, a Yayoi Settlement in Northern Kyushu. *Monumenta Nipponica*, 46(2), 211–235.

Barraclough, R. (2021). *Australian Outlook*, October 3.

Bausch, I. R. (2019). Adornments at the Odake Shell Midden: Perceptions of Early Jōmon Hunter-Gatherer Gender and Identities. In S. A. Lullo and L. V. Wallace, eds., *The Art and Archaeology of Bodily Adornment*. London: Routledge, pp. 19–40.

Beckwith, C. I. (2023). *The Scythian Empire*. Princeton, NJ: Princeton University Press.

Blacker, C. (1975). *The Catalpa Bow: A Study of Shamanistic Practices in Japan*. London: Allen & Unwin.

Boas, F. (1912). Changes in Bodily Form of Descendants of Immigrants. *American Anthropology*, 14(3), 530–562.

Broadbridge, A. F. (2018). *Women and the Making of the Mongol Empire*. Cambridge: Cambridge University Press.

Brown, J. (1989). The Beginnings of Pottery as an Economic Process. In S. van der Leeuw and R. Torrence, eds., *What's New: A Closer Look at the Process of Innovation*. London: Unwin Hyman, pp. 203–224.

Brumfiel, E. (2007). Review, Gender and Chinese Archaeology. *Asian Perspectives*, 46(1), 237–242.

Bunker, E. C. (1978). Gold Crowns in Korea, Japan, and Peru. *Art and Archaeology Research Papers* 13, 59–60.

Byington, M., ed. (2008). *Early Korea, Vol. 1: Reconsidering Early Korean History through Archaeology*. Cambridge, MA: Korea Institute at Harvard University.

(2009). *Early Korea, Vol. 2: The Samhan Period in Korean History*. Cambridge, MA: Korea Institute at Harvard University.

(2012). *Early Korea, Vol. 3: The Rediscovery of Kaya in History and Archaeology*. Cambridge, MA: Korea Institute at Harvard University.

Cascone, S. (2020). Archaeologists Have Discovered the Skeletons of "Badass" Warrior Women in Mongolia, Dating Back to the Period of Mulan. Art World. Art Net.com, May 13. https://news.artnet.com/art-world/mongolian-warrior-women-skeletons-mulan-1860144 (accessed March 10, 2022).

Chang Hsun 張珣 (1995). 女神信仰與媽祖崇拜的比較研究 (Two Comparative Approaches for the Study of the Cult of Matsu in Taiwan). 中央研究院民族學研究所集刊 (*Bulletin of the Institute of Ethnology Academia Sinica*), 79, 185–203.

Chen Jianli 陈建立, Chen Tiemei 陈铁梅, and Jia Changming 贾昌明 (2013). 从随葬工具的性别关联探讨中国新石器时代的性别分工 (Discussing the Gender Division of Labor in China's Neolithic Age from the Perspective of the Gender Relationship of Burial Tools). 南方文物 (*Southern Cultural Relics*), (02), 39–48.

Chen Po-chan 陈伯桢 (2009). 台湾民族考古学的回顾 (A Review of Ethnoarchaeology in Taiwan). 边疆民族考古与民族考古学集刊 (*Frontier Ethnic Archaeology and Ethnoarchaeology Collection*), (1), 231–244.

Chen, Y. C. (2021). Gender Identity, National Identity and the Right to Self-Determination: The Peculiar Case of Taiwan. In I. C. Jaramillo and L. Carlson, eds., *Trans Rights and Wrongs*. Ius Comparatum – Global Studies in Comparative Law, vol. 54, 133–148. Cham: Springer International Publishing. http://dx.doi.org/10.1007/978-3-030-68494-5_8 (accessed October 5, 2023).

Chen Yu-pei 陳有貝 (2015). 史前臺灣的人身裝飾品研究 (A Study on Body Ornaments in Prehistorical Taiwan). 國立臺灣博物館學刊 (*Journal of National Taiwan Museum*), 68(1), 19–24.

Cheong, S. H. (1998). The New Cultural Movement for Korean Women: Women's Studies in the Early 1920s. In The Research Institute of Asian Women, ed., *Korean Women and Culture*. Seoul: The Research Institute of Asian Women, pp. 97–120.

Chiang Bien 蔣斌 and Li Ching-yi 李靜怡 (1995). 北部排灣族家屋的空間結構與意義 (The Spatial Configuration of Northern Paiwan Houses and Its Significance). In 黃應貴編 Huang Y. K. ed., 空間、力與社會 (*Space, Power, and Society*). 臺北 Taipei:中央研究院民族學研究所 (Institute of Ethnology, Academia Sinica), pp. 167–212.

Chiang Chih-hua 江芝華 (2008). 考古學的家屋社會研究 (The Archaeology of House Societies). 考古人類學學刊 (*Journal of Archaeology and Anthropology*), (68), 109–136.

(2020). 考古學裡的性別研究 (Gender Studies in Archaeology). 婦研縱横 (*Forum on Women's and Gender Studies*), (112), 6–9.

Chiu Hung-lin 邱鴻霖 (2010). 臺灣史前時代拔齒習俗的社會意義研究: 以鐵器時代石橋遺址蔦松文化為例 (The Social Meaning of Ritual Tooth Ablation Behavior in Prehistoric Taiwan: A Case Study at the Shihchiao Site from the Iron-Age Niaosung Culture). 考古人類學刊 (*Journal of Archaeology and Anthropology*), (73), 1–59.

Choi, S. K. (1986). Formation of Women's Movement in Korea: From the Enlightenment Period to 1910. In S. W. Chung, ed., *Challenges for Women: Women's Studies in Korea*. Seoul: Ewha Womans University Press.

Choy, K. C., Yun, H. Y., Kim, S. H., Jung, S. S., Fuller, B. T., and Kim, D. W. (2021). Isotopic Investigation of Skeletal Remains at Imdang Tombs Reveals High Consumption of Game Bird and Social Stratification in Ancient Korea. *Scientific Reports*, 11, 22551. www.nature.com/articles/s41598-021-01798-y.

Chung Kuo-feng 鐘國風 (2020). 性別身份的文化形成過程:阿美族Lidaw社船祭成年禮的性別考古學視野 (The Process of Cultural Formation of Gender Identity: A Gender Archaeological Perspective on the Rite of Passage of the Ami Litaw Boat Festival). 婦研縱橫 (*Forum on Women's and Gender Studies*), (112), 22–31.

Conkey, M. and Spector, J., eds. (1984). Archaeology and the Study of Gender. *Advances in Archaeological Method and Theory*, 7, 1–38. www.jstor.org/stable/20170176 (accessed January 31, 2023).

Crawford, M. H. and Leonard, W. R. (2002). The Biological Diversity of Herding Populations: An Introduction. In W. R. Leonard and M. H. Crawford, eds., *Human Biology of Pastoral Populations*. Cambridge: Cambridge University Press, pp. 1–9.

Du Jinping 杜金鹏 (1995). 纵横交织的阴阳网络-夏商时期的男女社会关系 (The Network of Yin and Yang: Gender Relations in the Xia and Shang). In Ma Jiayin 闵家胤, ed., 阳刚与阴柔的变奏-两性关系和社会模式 (*Variations of Masculinity and Femininity: Gender Relations and Social Patterns*). Beijing: Zhongguo Shehui Kexueyuan Chubanshe, pp. 93–133.

Embassy (Embassy of the People's Republic of China in the United States of America) (2022). China Unveils Its Top 10 Archaeological Discoveries of 2021. Embassy of the People's Republic of China in the United States of America (website), April 1. http://us.china-embassy.gov.cn/eng/zggs/202204/t20220401_10658425.htm (accessed January 2, 2023).

Eng, J. T. (2013). Vertebral Joint Disease and Trauma with Horse Riding among Ancient Mongolian Pastoralists. *American Journal of Physical Anthropology* (Suppl.), 151–220.

(2016). A Bioarchaeological Study of Osteoarthritis among Populations of Northern China and Mongolia during the Bronze Age to Iron Age Transition to Nomadic Pastoralism. *Quaternary International*, 405, 172–185. http://dx.doi.org/10.1016/j.quaint.2015.07.072 (accessed September 20, 2024).

Erdene, M. (2013). A Nonmetric Comparative Study of Past and Contemporary Mongolian and Northeast Asian Crania. In K. Pechenkina and M. Oxenham, eds., *Bioarchaeology of East Asia: Movement, Contact, Health*. Gainesville: University Press of Florida, pp. 110–143. https://ebookcentral.proquest.com/lib/pitt-ebooks/reader.action?docID=1207189 (accessed March 10, 2022).

Ewha (n.d.). About Ewha. History/Symbols. Ewha Womans University (website). www.ewha.ac.kr›ewhaen›intro›history02-1 (accessed January 2, 2023).

Fang Lixia 方利霞 (2021). 中原地区商周墓葬随葬生产工具研究 (Research on the Production Tools of the Shang and Zhou Tombs in the Central Plains). Unpublished dissertation, Mentor: Zhang Guoshuo 张国硕, Zhengzhou University.

Farris, C. S. (2004). Women's Liberation under "East Asian Modernity" in China and Taiwan: Historical, Cultural, and Comparative Perspectives. In C. S. Farris, A. Lee, and M. A. Rubinstein, eds., *Women in the New Taiwan: Gender Roles and Gender Consciousness in a Changing Society*. Taiwan in the Modern World. Armonk, NY: M. E. Sharpe, pp. 325–376.

Farris, C. S., Lee, A., and Rubinstein, M. A. (2004). *Women in the New Taiwan: Gender Roles and Gender Consciousness in a Changing Society*. Taiwan in the Modern World. Armonk, NY: M. E. Sharpe.

Fawcett, C. (1996). Nationalism and Postwar Japanese Archaeology. In P. L. Kohl and C. Fawcett, eds., *Nationalism, Politics and the Practice of Archaeology*. Cambridge: Cambridge University Press, pp. 232–246.

Fijn, N. (2011). *Living with Herds: Human–Animal Coexistence in Mongolia*. Cambridge: Cambridge University Press.

Flad, R. K. (2023). Long Distance Influences and Local Adoption: Technological Changes in Ritual and Economy in Late Prehistoric Northwest China. In A. Hein, R. K. Flad, and B. Miller, eds., *The Art and Archaeology of Ritual and Economy in East Asia: Essays in Honor of Lothar von Falkenhausen*. Los Angeles, CA: Cotsen Institute of Archaeology Press at UCLA, pp. 197–221.

Friedman, S. and Chen, C. (2023). Same-Sex Marriage Legalization and the Stigmas of LGBT Co-parenting in Taiwan. *Law & Social Inquiry*, 48(2), 660–688.

Fujimura Junko 藤村淳子 (1996). 日本考古学とジェンダ (Japanese Archaeology and Gender). 女性史学 (*Women's History*), (6), 83–89.

(1998). ジェンダ一考古学–男性=狩猟者という神話 (Gender Archaeology: The Myth of Men = Hunters). 新書館編 (In Shinshokan, ed.), 大航海 : 歴史-文学-思想 (*The Voyage: History–Literature–Thought*), vol. 22, pp. 70–74.

Funahashi, K. (2022). Gender Expression from the Jōmon to Yayoi Periods in Western Japan: A Case Study of Ritual Tooth Extraction. *Japanese Journal of Archaeology*, 9(2), 145–172.

Grayson, J. H. (2015). Tan'gun and Chumong: The Politics of Korean Foundation Myths. *Folklore*, 126 (December), 253–265.

Gegel, L. (2020). Two "Warrior Women" from Ancient Mongolia May Have Helped Inspire the Ballad of Mulan. LiveScience, May 8. www.livescience.com/mongolia-warrior-women-mulan.html (accessed February 10, 2022).

Geng Chao 耿超 (2013). 殷墟族墓地中的"夫妇合葬墓"及相关问题 ("Joint Burial of Husband and Wife" and Related Issues in Yinxu Cemetery). 首都师范大学学报 (社会科学版 (*Journal of Capital Normal University* [*Social Science Edition*]), (02), 35–39.

(2014). 晋侯墓地的性别考察 (Gender Investigation of the Jinhou Cemetery). 中原文物 (*Central Plains Cultural Relics*), (03), 36–43.

Gould, S. J. (1981). *The Mismeasure of Man*. New York: W. W. Norton and Company.

Greaves, A. (2020). Women in the Early Mongol Empire: Female Types in the *Secret History of the Mongols*. Honors thesis, Brigham Young University. https://scholarsarchive.byu.edu/cgi/viewcontent.cgi?article=1119&context=studentpub_uht (accessed February 10, 2022).

Grier, C. and Kim, J. S. (2012). Resource Control and the Development of Political Economies in Small-Scale Societies: Contrasting Prehistoric Southwestern Korea and the Coast Salish Region of Northwestern North America. *Journal of Anthropological Research*, 68(1), 1–34.

Haboush, J. H. K. (2008). The Vanished Women of Korea: The Anonymity of Texts and the Historicity of Subjects. In A. Walthall, ed., *Servants of the Dynasty: Palace Women in World History*. Berkeley: University of California Press, pp. 280–298.

Habu, J. (2004). *Ancient Jōmon of Japan*. Cambridge: Cambridge University Press.

Habu, J. and Fawcett, C. (1999). Jōmon Archaeology and the Representation of Japanese Origins. *Antiquity*, 73(281), 587–593.

Hein, A., d'Alpoim Guedes, J., Lin, K.-c., and Teng, M. (2023). Female Scholars and Their Contributions to Chinese Archaeology. In S. L. Lopez Varela, ed., *Women in Archaeology: Intersectionalities in Practice Worldwide*. Cham: Springer, pp. 559–590. https://link.springer.com/chapter/10.1007/978-3-031-27650-7_28 (accessed April 6, 2024).

Higham, C. (2002). Women in the Prehistory of Mainland Southeast Asia. In S. M. Nelson and M. Rosen-Ayalon, eds., *In Pursuit of Gender: Worldwide Archaeological Approaches*. Walnut Creek, CA: AltaMira, pp. 207–224.

Holliman, S. E. (2011). Sex and Gender in Biological Research: Theory, Method and Interpretation. In S. C. Argawal and B. A. Glencross, eds., *Social Bioarchaeology*, Malden, MA: Wiley-Blackwell, pp. 150–182.

Honeychurch, W. (2014). Alternative Complexities: The Archaeology of Pastoral Nomadic States. *Journal of Archaeological Research*, 22(4), 277–326.

Hou Kan 侯侃 (2017). 山西榆次高校园区先秦墓葬人骨研究 (Research on the Human Skeletons from the Tombs of the Pre-Qin Period Excavated in the Higher Education Park in Yuci, Shanxi). Unpublished dissertation, Mentor: Zhu Hong 朱泓, Jilin University.

Hsieh Kuo-pin 謝國斌 (2011). 臺灣族群研究的發展 (The Development of Ethnic Studies in Taiwan). 臺灣原住民族研究學報 (*Journal of the Taiwan Indigenous Studies Association*), 1(1), 1–27.

Huang Xiurong 黄秀蓉 (2011). 论大溪墓葬与史前土家族区域社会性别关系 (On the Relationship between Daxi Tombs and Prehistoric Tujia Regional Social Gender). 西南大学学报 (社会科学版 (*Journal of Southwest University* [*Social Science Edition*]), 37(02), 156–162 + 193.

Hung, H. and Carson, M. (2014). Foragers, Fishers and Farmers: Origins of the Taiwanese Neolithic. *Antiquity*, 88(342), 1115–1131.

Igarashi, Y. (2022). Fertility and Survivorship in the Jōmon and Yayoi Periods Estimated from Human Bones. *Japanese Journal of Archaeology*, 9(2), 173–188.

Ikawa-Smith, F. (1980). Current Issues in Japanese archaeology. *American Scientist*, 68, 134–145.

(1988). Kamegoaka Social Networks. Paper delivered at the Annual Meeting of the Society for American Archaeology, Phoenix, Arizona, April.

Ikawa-Smith, F. and Habu, J. (2002). Gender in Japanese Archaeology. In S. M. Nelson and M. Rosen-Ayalon, eds., *In Pursuit of Gender, Worldwide Archaeological Approaches*. Walnut Creek, CA: AltaMira, pp. 323–54.

Imai Takashi 今井堯 (1982). 古墳時代前期における女性の地位 (The Status of Women in the Early Kofun Period). 歴史評論 (*Historical Journal*), (383), 2–24.

Izumori Kō 泉森皎 (1985). 刀剣出土状態の検討—刀剣の呪的性格の理解のために— (Examination of the Condition of Excavated Swords: For Understanding the Magical Nature of Swords). 末永先生米寿記念献呈論文集 (*Studies Dedicated to Professor Suenaga on the Occasion of His Eighty-Eighth Birthday*). 乾 末永先生米寿記念会 (Suenaga-sensei Beiju Kinenkai), 奈良 Nara, pp. 393–435.

Jia Ying 贾莹 (2006). 山西浮山桥北及乡宁内阳垣先秦时期人骨研究 (Research on Human Bones in the Pre-Qin Period in the North of Fushan Bridge and Neiyangyuan in Xiangning, Shanxi). Unpublished dissertation, Mentor: Zhu Hong 朱泓, Jilin University.

Jiang Yi-huah 江宜樺 (1998). 當前臺灣國家認同論述之反省 (Reflections on the Discourses of National Identity in Taiwan). 臺灣社會研究季刊 (*Taiwan Social Research Quarterly*), 29(3), 163–229.

Joyce, R. and Claassen, C. (1997). Women in the Ancient Americas: Archaeologists, Gender, and the Making of Prehistory. In C. Claassen and R. Joyce, eds., *Women in Prehistory: North America and Mesoamerica*. Philadelphia: University of Pennsylvania Press, pp. 1–14.

JUIAF (Jilin University International Academic Forum) (2008). 女考古学家的思考与实践 (Thoughts and Practices of Female Archaeologists), 国际学术动态 (*International Academic Developments*), (5), 31–32.

Kendall, L. (1996). Korean Shamans and the Spirits of Capitalism. *American Anthropologist*, 98(3), 512–527.

Keyser, C., Zvéigorosky, V., Gonzalez, A., Fausser, J.-L., Jagorel, F., Gérard, P., Turbat Tsagaan, Duchesne, S., Crubézy, E. and Ludes, B. (2020). Genetic Evidence Suggests a Sense of Family, Parity and Conquest in the Xiongnu Iron Age Nomads of Mongolia. *Human Genetics*, 140(2), 349–358. https://pubmed.ncbi.nlm.nih.gov/32734383/ (accessed March 10, 2022).

Keyser-Tracqui, C., Crubézy, E., and Ludes, B. (2003). Nuclear and Mitochondrial DNA Analysis of a 2,000-Year-Old Necropolis in the Egyin Gol Valley of Mongolia. *American Journal of Human Genetics*, 73(2), 247–260. https://pubmed.ncbi.nlm.nih.gov/12858290/ (accessed March 10, 2022).

Khayutina, M. (2014). Marital Alliances and Affinal Relatives (sheng 甥 and hungou 婚購) in the Society and Politics of Zhou China in the Light of Bronze Inscriptions. *Early China*, (37), 1–61.

(2017). Tombs of the Rulers of the Peng and Relationships between Zhou and Northern Non-Zhou Lineages. In E. Shaughnessy, ed., *Imprints of Kingship: Studies of Recently Discovered Inscriptions from Ancient China*. Hong Kong: University of Hong Kong Press, pp. 71–132.

Kidder, J. E. (1987). The Fujinoki Tomb and Its Grave-Goods. *Monumenta Nipponica*, 42(1), 57–87.

Kim Bumcheol 김범철 (2011). Ch'ŏngdonggishidae Chŏn'gi Chugŏ Yangsanggwa Kagu Baltalchugi: Hosŏchiyŏk yŏksamdong mit Hŭnam-ri yuhyŏng Ch'wirakŭl Chungshimŭro 青銅器時代 前期 住居樣相과 家口發達週期: 호서지역 驛三洞 및 欣岩里類型 聚落을 중심으로 (Dwelling Patterns and Household Developmental Cycle during the Early Bronze Age: With Special Reference to Yeoksam-dong and Heunam-ri Type Settlements of the Hoseo Region). *Han'guk sanggosa hakpo* 韓國上古史學報 (*Journal of the Korean Ancient Historical Society*), (72), 31–60.

Kim, B. (2015). Socioeconomic Development in the Bronze Age: Archaeological Understanding of the Transition from the Early to Middle Bronze Age, South Korea. *Asian Perspectives*, 54(1), 144–184.

Kim, C. K. and Lee, U. C. (1975). *A Report on the Excavation of Tombs at Hwangnam-dong, Kyongju* [Korean, English summary]. Singapore: Yongnam University Museum.

Kim, J., Yang, U. A., Huh, H. R., and Yoo, H. R. (2000). A Study on the History of Women's Education in Korea. *Women's Studies Forum*, 18, 45–65.

Kim, J. E., Jeon, H. R., Choi, J. P., Blazyte, A. S., Yeonsu Jeon, Y. S., Kim, J. I., Hyunran, J., Ohashi, Tokunaga K. , Sugano, S., Fucharoen, S., Fahd Al-Mulla, and Jong B. (2020). The Origin and Composition of Korean Ethnicity Analyzed by Ancient and Present-Day Genome Sequences. *Genome Biology and Evolution*, 12(5), 553–565. https://doi.org/10.1093/gbe/evaa062 (accessed October 12, 2022).

Kim, W. Y. (1982). The Homeland of Korean Culture. *Korea Journal*, 22(9), 247–275.

Kim, W. Y. and Pearson, R. (1977). Three Royal Tombs: New Discoveries in Korean Archaeology. *Archaeology*, 30(5), 302–313.

Kim, Y. C., ed. And trans. (1976). *Women of Korea: A History from Ancient Times to 1945*. Seoul: Ewha Womans University Press.

Kinney, A. B., ed. And trans. (2014). *Exemplary Women of Early China: The* Lienü *zhuan of Liu Xiang*. New York: Columbia University Press.

(2018). Women in Early China: Views from the Archaeological Record. In P. Golden, ed., *Routledge Handbook of Early Chinese History*. London: Routledge, pp. 373–391.

Ko Yu-chieh 柯渝婕 (2020). 愛美是女人的天性?重思蔦松遺址中的「裝飾品」陶環 (Is It a Woman's Nature to Love Beauty? Rethinking the Ornamental Pottery Rings in the Ruins of the Niaosung Site). 婦研縱橫 (*Forum on Women's and Gender Studies*), (112), 32–39.

Kobayashi Seiji 小林青樹 (2007). 弥生絵画の象徴考古学一身体・ジェンダー・戦争一 (Symbolic Archeology of Yayoi Paintings: Body, Gender, and War). 上代文化 (*Ancient Culture*), (40), 17–30.

Kuo, S.-c. (2023). *Tracing the History of Contemporary Taiwan's Aboriginal Groups: From the Periphery to the Centre*. Routledge Studies in the Early History of Asia. London: Routledge. https://doi.org/10.4324/9781003241331 (accessed August 5, 2023).

Lee, B. Y. (2008). *Women in Korean History*. Seoul: Ewha Womans University Press.

Lee Hyong-gu (2018). 춘천 중도유적과 그 의미 (Jungdo Historic Site in Chuncheon and Its Significance). 광장일지 (*Journal of Gwangjang*), (219), 248–250.

Lee, J. Y., Miller, B. K., Bayarsaikhan, J., Johannesson, E., Ventresca Miller, A., Warinner, X., and Jeong, Choongwon (2023). Genetic Population Structure of the Xiongnu Empire at Imperial and Local Scales. *Science Advances*, 9(15). www.science.org/doi/10.1126/sciadv.adf3904 (accessed April 30, 2023).

Lee, R. J. and Bale, M. T. (2016). Social Change and Household Geography in Mumun Period South Korea. *Journal of Anthropological Research*, 72(2), 178–199.

Li Changying 李长盈 (2015). 山东胶州三里河遗址大汶口文化墓葬的时空结构 (The Spatiotemporal Structure of the Dawenkou Cultural Tombs at the Sanlihe Site in Jiaozhou, Shandong). 东南文化 (*Southeast Culture*), (05), 56–67.

Li, Xinquan (2016). The Shijia Cemetery at Fushun. In Mark E. Byington, ed., *The History and Archaeology of the Koguryo Kingdom*. Early Korea Project Occasional Series. Cambridge, MA: Korea Institute at Harvard University.

Li Yaohui 李耀辉 (2021). 大汶口文化拔牙习俗原因及意义探究 (Reasons and Significance of Tooth Extraction Custom in the Dawenkou Culture). 文物鉴定与鉴赏 (*Identification and Appreciation of Cultural Relics*), (19), 42–45.

Lin Kuei-chen 林圭偵 (2020). 不存在的邊地婦女 (Nonexistent Frontier Women). 婦研縱橫 (*Forum on Women's and Gender Studies*), (112), 54–63.

Linduff, K. M. (2006). Why Have Siberian Artefacts Been Excavated Inside the Ancient Chinese Dynastic Borders? In A. Smith, D. Peterson, and L. M. Popova, eds., *Beyond the Steppe and the Sown: Integrating Local and Global Visions*. Gocha Tsetskhladze, *Colloquia Pontica*. Leiden: Brill, pp. 358–370.

(2008). The Gender and Power of Luxury and Power among the Xiongnu. In K. M. Linduff and K. S. Rubinson, eds., *Are All Warriors Male? Gender Roles on the Ancient Eurasian Steppe*. Latham, MD: AltaMira Press, pp. 175–212.

(2022). Linking Violence and Sexuality in Revolutionary China: Red Detachment of Women (红色娘子军 1964). Paris: Centre de recherche sur l'Extrême-Orient de Sourbonne-Paris. https://creops.hypotheses.org/linking-violence-and-sexuality-in-revolutionary-china (accessed January 2, 2023).

Linduff, K. M. and Rubinson, K. S. (2022). *Pazyryk Culture up in the Altai*. London: Routledge.

Linduff, K. M. and Sun, Y., eds. (2004). *Gender and Chinese Archaeology*. Walnut Creek, CA: AltaMira.

Lin Jialin 林嘉琳 (Linduff, K. M.) and Sun Yan 孙岩, eds. (2006). 性别研究与中国考古学 (*Gender and Chinese Archaeology*). 北京大学震旦古代文明研究中心 (Aurora Center for the Study of Ancient Civilizations) 北京大学 (Beijing University). Beijing: Science Press.

Liu, L. (2004). *The Chinese Neolithic: Trajectories to Early States*, Cambridge: Cambridge University Press. (Beijing: Cultural Relics Press, 2007 [in Chinese]).

Liu, L. and Chen, X. (2012). *The Archaeology of China: From the Late Paleolithic to the Early Bronze Age*. Cambridge: Cambridge University Press.

Liu, L. and Chen, X. (2014). *Exemplary Women of Early China: The Lienü zhuan of Liu Xiang*. New York: Columbia University Press.

Liu Nan 刘楠 (2021). 几何形态测量学在考古中的应用 (Application of Geometric Morphometry in Archaeology). Unpublished dissertation, Jilin University.

Liu Pi-chen 劉璧榛 (2007). 稻米、野鹿與公雞:噶瑪蘭人的食物、權力與性別象徵 (Rice, Deer and Rooster: Foods, Power and Gender Symbols among the Kavalan of Taiwan). 考古人類學刊 (*Journal of Archaeology and Anthropology*), (67), 43–70.

(2008). 身體、女神與祖靈:噶瑪蘭女巫師研究 (Bodies, Goddesses, and Ancestral Spirits: A Study of Kamalan Women Shamans). In 胡國楨 (Peter Hu), 丁立偉 (Li-wei Ting), eds., 原住民巫術與基督宗教 (*Aboriginal Shamans and Christianity*). 臺北 Taipei: 光啟文化事業 (Guangqi Cultural Undertakings), pp. 64–82.

(2020). Shamanism and Gender Construction among the Kavalan of Taiwan Men and Women's Illness Caused by Different Spirits. In D. Torri and S. Roche, eds., *The Shamaness in Asia: Gender, Religion and the State*. Milton Park: Taylor & Francis, pp. 208–224.

Liu Yi-chang 劉益昌 (2006). 臺灣考古學與原住民研究 (The Discipline of Taiwanese Archaeology and Studies of Indigenous Groups). 國立臺灣大學考古人類學刊 (*Bulletin of the Department of Anthropology of National Taiwan University*), (66), 70–93.

(2019). 典藏臺灣史 (一) 史前人群與文化 (*Taiwan History Collection, Vol. 1: Peoples and Cultures of the Prehistoric Period*). 臺北 Taipei: 玉山社 (Yushan Society).

Lu, H. Y. (2004). Imagining Women, Imagining Modernity: Constructing "New Women" in Colonial Taiwan. In C. S. Ferris, A. Lee, and M. A. Rubinstein, eds., *Women in the New Taiwan: Gender Roles and Gender Consciousness in a Changing Society*. Taiwan in the Modern World. Armonk, NY: M. E. Sharpe, pp. 76–98.

Lu Jou-chun 盧柔君 (2020). 故事與說故事的人:日本考古學論域中性別觀的更迭與限制 (Stories and Storytellers: Changes and Limitations of Gender Perspectives in the Field of Japanese Archaeology). 婦研縱橫 (*Forum on Women's and Gender Studies*), (112), 40–53.

Ma Jiayin 闵家胤, ed. (1995). 阳刚与阴柔的变奏-两性关系和社会模式 (*Variations of Masculinity and Femininity: Gender Relations and Social Patterns*). Beijing: Zhongguo Shehui Kexueyuan Chubanshe.

Matsumoto Naoko 松本直子 (1998). ジェンダー考古学の現在 (Gender Archaeology Today). 女性学年報 (*Annals of Women Study*), (19), 43–51.

(2008). ジェンダー (Gender). In 小杉康 Y. Kosugi, ed., 縄文時代の考古学 10 (*Archaeology of the Jōmon Period*, vol. 10). Tokyo: 同成社 Doseisha, pp. 133–144.

(2010). Women of Prehistoric Japan. In Yangjin Pak ed., *Proceedings of an International Conference in Daejon, Korea: Women of Ancient East Asia*. November 2009. Daejon: Paekche Research Society, pp. 79–85.

(2017). ジェンダー教育と考古学 (Gender Education and Archaeology). In 吉田泰幸 Yasuyuki Yoshida, ed., 文化資源学セミナー「考古学と現代社会」2013–16 (*Seminar on Cultural Resources: Archaeology and Contemporary Society* 2013–2016, ed.). Tokyo: 国際文化資源学研究センター (International Research Center for Cultural Resources), pp. 167–182.

(2021). 縄文-弥生時代の性差と考古学 (Gender Differences and Archaeology of the Jōmon and Yayoi Periods). 月刊考古学ジャーナル (*Monthly Journal of Archaeology*), (762), 19–22.

Matsumoto, N. and Mitsumoto, J. (2022). Guest Editors' Introduction. *Japanese Journal of Archaeology*, 9(2), 143–144.

Meller, H. (2016). Jongdo Excavation. *Archäologie in Deutschland*, Editorial 4/16, 1.

Migishima Kazuo 右島和夫, Wakasa Tōru 若狭徹, and Uchiyama Toshiyuki 内山敏行 (2011). 古墳時代毛野の実像 (Actual Image of Kenu from the Kofun Period). 季刊考古学別冊17号 (Kikan kōkogaku, 17, *Quarterly Archaeology*, Special Issue No. 17). 東京: 雄山閣 (Tokyo: Yūzankaku).

Miller, B. (2024). *Xiongnu: The World's First Nomadic Empire*, Oxford: Oxford University Press.

Miller, B. and Brosseder, U. (2017). Global Dynamics in Local Processes of Iron Age Inner Asia. In T. Hodos, ed., *The Routledge Handbook of Archaeology and Globalization*. New York: Routledge, pp. 470–487.

Mitsumoto, Jun (2019). Beyond Heteronormativity: Queer Archaeology in Japan. Paper presented at the Archaeological Research Facility, University of California, Berkeley, February 11, Berkeley, CA.

Mitsumoto, Jun (2022). Bodily Representation and Cross-Dressing in the Yayoi and Kofun Periods. *Japanese Journal of Archaeology*, 9(2), 189–210.

Mizoguchi, K. (2013). *The Archaeology of Japan: From the Earliest Rice Farming Villages to the Rise of the State*. Cambridge: Cambridge University Press.

Molony, B. (2004). Frameworks of Gender: Feminism and Nationalism in Twentieth-Century Asia. In T. A. Meade and M. E. Wiesner-Hanks, eds., *A Companion to Gender History*. Oxford: Blackwell, pp. 513–539.

Murphy, E. M., Schulting, R., Beer, N., Chistov, Y., Kasparov, A., and Pshenitsyna, M. (2013). Iron Age Pastoral Nomadism and Agriculture in the Eastern Eurasian Steppe: Implications from Dental Palaeopathology and Stable Carbon and Nitrogen Isotopes. *Journal of Archaeological Science*, (40), 2547–2560.

Muyard, F. (2012). The Formation of Taiwan's New National Identity since the End of the 1980s. In D. Blundell, ed., *Taiwan since Martial Law: Society, Politics, Economy*. Shung Ye Museum of Formosan Aborigines, University of California – Berkeley, and National Taiwan University Press, pp. 297–366.

Nagamine, M. (1986). Clay Figurines and Jomon Society. In R. J. Pearson, ed., *Windows on the Japanese Past*. Ann Arbor: Center for Japanese Studies at the University of Michigan, pp. 255–266.

Nahm, A. C. (1989). Korean Women's Modernization Movement, 1896–1945. In *Proceedings of the Tenth International Symposium on Asian Studies*, Vol. 2. Hong Kong: Asian Research Service, n.p.

Nakazawa, Y. (2010). Dual Nature in the Creation of Disciplinary Identity: A Socio-historical Review of Palaeolithic Archaeology in Japan. *Asian Perspectives*, 49(2), 231–250. https://muse-jhu-edu.pitt.idm.oclc.org/article/468262/pdf (accessed September 12, 2024).

Nelson, S. (1986). The Social Dimension of Burials in Prehistoric Korea. *Proceedings of the 7th International Symposium on Asian Studies, 1985*. Hong Kong: Asian Research Service, pp. 247–256.

(1990). Diversity of the Upper Paleolithic "Venus" Figurines and Archaeological Mythology. In S. Nelson and A. Kehoe, eds., *Powers of Observation, Alternative Views in Archaeology*. Archaeological Papers of the American

Anthropological Association, 2(1). Arlington, VA: American Anthropological Association, pp. 11–22.

(1991a). The "Goddess Temple" and the Status of Women at Niuheliang, China. In D. Walde and N. Willows, eds., *The Archaeology of Gender*. Proceedings of the 22nd Annual Chacmool Conference of the Archaeological Association of the University of Calgary. Calgary: The University of Calgary Archaeological Association, pp. 302–308.

(1991b). The Statuses of Women in Ko-Shilla: Evidence from Archaeology and Historical Documents. *Korea Journal*, 31(2), 101–107.

(1993). Gender Hierarchies and the Queens of Silla. In B. D. Miller, ed., *Sex and Gender Hierarchies*. Cambridge: Cambridge University Press, pp. 272–315.

(1995). Introduction. In S. Nelson, ed., *The Archaeology of Northeast China: Beyond the Great Wall*. London: Routledge Press, pp. 1–18.

(1996). Ideology and the Formation of an Early State in Northeast China. In H. Claessen and J. Oosten, eds., *Ideology and the Early State*. Leiden: Brill, pp. 153–169.

(1997). *Gender in Archaeology: Analyzing Power and Prestige*. Walnut Creek, CA: AltaMira Press.

(2002). Ideology, Power, and Gender: Emergent Complex Society in Northeast China. In S. Nelson and M. Rosen Ayalon, eds., *In Pursuit of Gender: Worldwide Archaeological Perspectives*. Walnut Creek, CA: AltaMira Press, pp. 73–80.

ed. (2003). *Ancient Queens: Archaeological Explorations*. Walnut Creek, CA: AltaMira Press.

ed. (2006). *Handbook of Gender in Archaeology*. Walnut Creek, CA: AltaMira Press.

(2008a). Horses and Gender in Korea: The Legacy of the Steppe on the Edge of Asia. In K. M. Linduff and K. S. Rubinson, eds., *Are All Warriors Male? Gender Roles on the Ancient Eurasian Steppe*. Lanham, MD: AltaMira Press, pp. 111–130.

(2008b). *Shamanism and the Origin of States: Spirit, Power, and Gender in East Asia*. Walnut Creek, CA: Left Coast Press.

(2013). Gender and Archeology in Coastal East Asia. In D. Bolger, ed., *A Companion to Gender Prehistory*. Chichester: John Wiley & Sons, pp. 330–350.

(2016). *Shamans, Queens and Figurines, The Development of Gender Archaeology*. Walnut Creek, CA: Left Coast Press.

Nelson, S. and Rosen-Ayalon, M., eds. (2002). *In Pursuit of Gender: Worldwide Archaeological Approaches*. Walnut Creek, CA: AltaMira Press.

Nie Ying 聂颖 (2022). 聂颖.新疆石河子十户窑墓群青铜 – 铁器时代人骨研究 (Bronze–Iron Age Human Bones in Shihezi Shihu Kiln Tombs, Xinjiang). Unpublished dissertation, Mentor: Zhu Hong 朱泓, Jilin University.

NUAC (Nanjing University Academic Conference) (2010). 女性考古与女性遗产 (Female Archaeology and Female Heritage). August 13–15.

Nyitray, V. L. (2004). Confucian Complexities: China, Japan, Korea, and Vietnam. In T. A. Meade and M. E. Wiesner-Hanks, eds., *A Companion to Gender History*. Oxford: Blackwell.

O'Hara, A. R. SJ (1971). *The Position of Women in Early China: According to the Lieh Nü Chuan (The Biographies of Chinese Women)*, 2nd ed. Taipei: Mei Ya Publications.

Okladnikov, A. (1981). *Art of the Amur: Ancient Art of the Russian Far East*. New York: Abrams.

Ōta-shi Kyōiku Iinkai (太田市教育委員会.) (2012). 塚廻り古墳群Tsukamawari Kohungun (Tsukawari Tumulus). 群馬県太田市: Gunma ken, Ōta-shi: 太田市教育委員会 文化財課 (Ōta-shi Kyōiku Iinkai Bunkazai-ka).

Pak, Y. (1988). The Origins of Silla Metal Work. *Orientations* (September), 44–53.

Park, J. (1990). Trailblazers in a Traditional World: Korea's First Women College Graduates, 1910–1945. *Social Science History*, 14(4), 533–558.

Pearson, R. J. (2006). Jomon Hot Spot: Increasing Sedentism in South-Western Japan in the Incipient Jomon (14,000–9250 cal. BC) and Earliest Jomon (9250–5300 cal. BC) Periods. *World Archaeology*, 38(2), 239–258.

(2023). *Taiwan Archaeology: Local Development and Cultural Boundaries in the China Seas*. Honolulu: University of Hawai'i Press.

Pechenkina, K. and Oxenham, M., eds., (2013). *Bioarchaeology of East Asia: Movement, Contact, Health*. Gainesville: University Press of Florida. https://ebookcentral.proquest.com/lib/pitt-ebooks/reader.action?docID=1207189 (accessed March 10, 2021).

Perrin, A. (2010). Images of Women in the Koguryo Painted Tombs. In Y. Pak, ed., *Women of Ancient East Asia: Proceedings of an International Conference in Daejon, Korea*. November 2009. Daejon: Paekche Research Society, pp. 95–103.

Pietrusewsky, M., Lauer, A., Tsang, C. H., Li, K. T., and Douglas, M. T. (2013). Dental Indicators of Health in Early Neolithic and Iron Age Skeletons from Taiwan. 南島研究學報 (*Journal of Austronesian Studies*), 4(2), 1–33. https://doi-org.pitt.idm.oclc.org/10.29884/JAS.201312_4(2).0001 (accessed April 10, 2023).

Piggott, J. (1997). *The Emergence of Japanese Kingship*. Palo Alto, CA: Stanford University Press.

(1999). Chiefdom Pairs and Co-rulers: Female Sovereignty in Early Japan. In H. Tonomura, A. Walthall, and W. Haruko, eds., *Women and Class in Japanese History*. Ann Arbor: Center for Japanese Studies at the University of Michigan, pp. 17–52.

Poo, M. (2018). *Daily Life in Ancient China*. Cambridge: Cambridge University Press.

Pu Wenqing 濮文清 (2018). 人类学视角下的中国性别考古学 (Chinese Gender Archaeology from the Perspective of Anthropology). Unpublished dissertation, Nanjing University.

Pyburn, A. (2004). Rethinking Complex Society. In K. A Pyburn, ed., *Engendering Civilization*. London: Routledge, pp. 1–46.

Qiao Yu 乔玉 (2014). 兴隆洼文化房屋内遗存所反映的性别问题 (Gender Issues Reflected in the Remains of Cultural Houses in Xinglongwa). 北方文物 (*Northern Cultural Relics*), (04), 23–27.

Qin Chang 秦畅 (2021). 性别考古学视角的新石器时代墓葬与社会分析 (Neolithic Tombs and Social Analysis from the Perspective of Gender Archaeology). Unpublished dissertation, Mentor: Yang Hua 杨华, Chongqing Normal University.

Rorex, R. (1974). *Eighteen Songs of a Nomad Flute: The Story of Lady Wen-Ch'i*. New York: Metropolitan Museum.

Rossabi, M. (n.d.). Women in Mongolia. https://en.wikipedia.org/wiki/Women_in_Mongolia (accessed March 10, 2022).

Sasse, W. (2001). Trying to Figure Out How Kings Became Kings in Silla. In Ok Yi, Daniel Bouchez, and Yun-ik Chang, eds., *Mélanges offerts à Li Ogg et Daniel Bouchez*, vol. 7. Paris: Centre d'études coréenes, pp. 229–244.

Seike Akira 清家章 (2010). 古墳時代の埋葬原理と親族構造 (*Burial Principles and Kinship Structure of the Kofun Period*). 吹田市Siuta City: 大阪大学出版会 Ōsaka University Press.

(2018). 古墳時代の首長位継承–女性首長論を中心に (Chieftain Succession in the Kofun Period: Focusing on the Theory of Female Chieftains). 法制史研究 (*Journal of Legal History*), (67), 223–236.

(2021). 古墳時代ジェンダー研究とDNA分析 (Gender Studies and DNA Analysis of the Kofun Period). 月刊考古学ジャーナル (*Monthly Journal of Archaeology*), (762), 11–14.

Shelach, G. (1999). *Leadership Strategies, Economic Activity, and Interregional Interaction: Social Complexity in Northeast China*. Boston, MA: Kluwer Academic and Plenum.

Shelach-Lavi, G. (2004). Marxist and Post-Marxist Paradigms for the Neolithic. In K. M. Linduff and Y. Sun, eds., *Gender and Chinese Archaeology*. Walnut Creek, CA: AltaMira, pp. 11–27.

(2015). *The Archaeology of Early China: From Prehistory to the Han Dynasty*. Cambridge: Cambridge University Press.

Shen, Shiau-Chi. (2022). Identity in Formation and Transformation: Dynamics of National Identity Change after Taiwan's Democratization. In P. C. Y. Chow, ed., *A Century of Development in Taiwan*. Cheltenham: Edward Elgar Publishing, pp. 73–93.

Shen Yafan 申亚凡, Zhao Yongsheng 赵永生, Fang Hui 方辉, and Chen Xuexiang 陈雪香 (2021). 济南大辛庄遗址商代居民的牙齿疾病 (Dental Diseases of Shang Dynasty Residents at the Daxinzhuang Site in Jinan). *Acta Anthropology*, 40(4), 628–643.

Sheng, L. (2002). Lee Teng-hui and the "Two-States" Theory. In L. J. Sheng ed., *China and Taiwan: Cross-Strait Relations under Chen Shui-bian* (China and Asia-Pacific). London: Zed Books, pp. 11–39.

Sun Haoran 孙浩然 (2019). 梁王城遗址大汶口文化墓葬相关问题探讨 (Discussion on the Related Issues of Dawenkou Cultural Tombs at the Liangwangcheng Site). 文物春秋 (*Cultural Relics Chunqiu*), 2(05), 12–20.

Sun Lei 孙蕾 (2013). 郑州汉唐宋墓葬出土人骨研究 (Research on Human Bones Unearthed from Tombs of the Han, Tang and Song Dynasties in Zhengzhou). Unpublished dissertation, Mentor: Zhu Hong 朱泓, Jilin University.

Sun, Y. (2021). *Many Worlds under One Heaven: Material Culture, Identity, and Power in the Northern Frontiers of the Western Zhou*. New York: Columbia University Press.

Sun Zhuo 孙卓 (2019). 西坡墓地初探 (A Preliminary Study on the Xipo Cemetery). 华夏考古 (*Huaxia Archaeology*), (01), 72–80.

Tang Xiaowen 唐晓雯 (2021). 唐新城长公主墓中女扮男装现象的性别考古学研究 (A Gendered Archaeological Study on the Phenomenon of Women Disguised as Men in the Tomb of the Chang Princess of Tang Xincheng). 浙江艺术职业学院学报 (*Journal of Zhejiang Art Vocational College*), 19(01), 108–112.

Teng Mingyu 滕铭予 (2018). 北京延庆葫芦沟墓地的布局与相关问题 (Layout and Related Issues of Hulugou Cemetery in Yanqing, Beijing). 考古 (*Archaeology*), (04), 82–90 + 2.

Tsang Cheng-hwa 臧振華 (1995). 臺灣考古 *The Archaeology of Taiwan*, 臺北文化資產叢書之52 (Taipei Cultural Assets Series No. 52). 臺北Taipei: 行政院文建會 (Council for Cultural Affairs, Executive Yuan).

(2005a). 從考古資料看蘭嶼雅美人的祖源問題 (On the Origin of the Yami People of Lanyu as Viewed from Archaeological Data). 南島研究學報 (*Journal of South Island Studies*), 1(1): 135–151.

(2005b). The Tapengkeng Culture sites in Taiwan. In L. Sagart, R. Blench, and A. Sanchez-Mazas, eds., *The Peopling of East Asia: Putting Together Archaeology, Linguistics, and Genetics*. London: Routledge Curzon, pp. 63–73.

Uchida Junko 内田純子 (2020). 城市化與性別化社會–以殷墟為例 (Urbanization and Gendered Society: A Case Study of Yin Xu). 婦研縱横 (*Forum on Women's and Gender Studies*), (112), 10–21.

Varutti, M. (2011). Toward Social Inclusion in Taiwan: Museums, Equality, and Indigenous Groups. In R. Sandell and E. Nightingale, eds., *Museums, Equality, and Social Justice*. London: Routledge.

Wang Chien-lung 王前龍 (2000). 國民中學《認識臺灣(社會篇)》教科書中之國家認同論述–從自由主義與民族主義的觀點來解析 (National Identity and the Textbooks of "Knowing Taiwan": Perspectives of Liberalism and Nationalism). 教育研究集刊 (*Journal of Education and Research*), (45), 139–172.

Wang Jianwen 王建文 (2012). 性别角色与社会习俗研究 – – 以贾湖遗址为例 (Research on Gender Roles and Social Customs: Taking Jiahu Site as an Example). *Shanghai Museum Collection*, (00), 436–462.

Wang Jianwen 王建文 and Zhang Tongxin 张童心 (2008). 墓葬习俗中的性别研究 – 以贾湖遗址为例 (Research on Gender in Burial Customs: Taking Jiahu Site as an Example). 四川文物 (*Sichuan Cultural Relics*), (06), 39–44.

Wang Jing 王静 (2021). 先秦两汉"形法"研究 (Research on "Form and Method" in the Pre-Qin and Han Dynasties). Unpublished dissertation, Mentor: Xi Wenqian 郗文倩, Fujian Normal University.

Wang Lusi 王路思 (2014). 侯马公路货运枢纽中心虒祁墓地人骨研究 (Research on Human Bones in Xiqi Cemetery in Houma Highway Freight Hub Center). Unpublished dissertation, Mentor: Zhang Quanchao 张全超, Jilin University.

Wang Minghui 王明辉, Jia Xiaobing贾笑冰, Li Xinwei 李新伟 et al. (2021). 科技助力考古学 – – 中国考古学百年纪念 (Scientific Technology Assists Archeology: Commemorating the Centenary of Chinese Archeology). 科学世界 (*Science World*), (10), 8–61.

Wang Shuai 王帅 (2021). 曲村墓地斂葬器物研究 (Research on Burial Artifacts in Qucun Cemetery). Unpublished dissertation, Shanxi University.

Wang Wei 王伟 (2012). 山西绛县横水西周墓地人骨研究 (Research on Human Bones in the Western Zhou Cemetery in Hengshui, Jiangxian

County, Shanxi Province). Unpublished dissertation, Mentor: Zhang Quanchao 张全超, Jilin University (吉林大学).

Wilcox, E. (2019). A Revolt from Within: Contextualizing Revolutionary Ballet. In E. Wilcox, *Revolutionary Bodies*. Berkeley: University of California Press. https://doi.org/10.1525/luminos.58 (accessed February 24, 2022).

Wright, J. S. (2016). Households without Houses: Mobility and Moorings on the Eurasian Steppe. *Journal of Anthropological Research*, 72(2), 133–157.

Wu, J. M. (2004). The Late Neolithic Cemetery at Dadianzi, Inner Mongolia Autonomous Region. In K. M. Linduff and S. Yan, eds., *Gender and Chinese Archaeology*. Walnut Creek, CA: AltaMira, pp. 47–94.

Wu Jui-man 吴瑞满 (2006). 墓葬习俗中的性别角色研究–以内蒙古自治区大甸子墓地为例 (The Late Neolithic Cemetery at Dadianzi, Inner Mongolia Autonomous Region). In Lin Jialin 林嘉琳 (Linduff, K. M.) and Sun Yan 孙岩, eds., 性别研究与中国考古学 (*Gender and Chinese Archaeology*), 北京大学震旦古代文明研究中心 (Aurora Center for the Study of Ancient Civilizations), 北京大学 (Beijing University). Beijing: Science Press, pp. 33–72.

Wu, X. L. (2004). Female and Male Status Displayed at the Maoqinggou Cemetery. In K. M. Linduff and Y. Sun, eds., *Gender and Chinese Archaeology*. Walnut Creek, CA: AltaMira, pp. 203–236.

(2017). *Material Culture, Power, and Identity in Ancient China*. Cambridge: Cambridge University Press.

Wu Xiaolong 吴霄龙 (2006). 毛庆沟墓地所体现的男性及女性社会地位: 继承的还是获取的 ? (Female and Male Status Displayed at the Maoqinggou Cemetery?). In Lin Jialin 林嘉琳 (Linduff, K. M.) and Sun Yan 孙岩, eds., 性别研究与中国考古学 (*Gender and Chinese Archaeology*), 北京大学震旦古代文明研究中心 (Aurora Center for the Study of Ancient Civilizations), 北京大学 (Beijing University). Beijing: Science Press, pp. 178–202.

Xi Jinping 习近平 (2020). 民族复兴 (National Rejuvenation). xinhuanet.com, September 9. www.xinhuanet.com/politics/2020-11/30/c_1126803588.htm (accessed January 31, 2022).

Xinhua (ed.) (2023). Xinhua Headlines: Key Takeaways from Xi's Diplomacy in 2023. https://english.news.cn/20231230/447200fdfc7141e8bbd8e9da5a5b9046/c.html.

Yang M. A., Fan X., Sun B., Chen C., Lang J, Ko Y.-C., Tsang C., Chiu H., Wang T., Bao Q., Wu X., Hajdinjak M., Ko A. M.-S., Ding M., Cao P., Yang R., Liu F., Nickel B., Dai Q., Feng X., Zhang L., Sun C., Ning C., Zeng W., Zhao Y., Zhang M., Gao X., Cui Y., Reich D., Stoneking M., Fu Q. (2020). Ancient

DNA Indicates Human Population Shifts and Admixture in Northern and Southern China. *Science*, 369(6501), 282–288.

Yang Su 杨愫 (2021). 对"性别考古学"在中国发展现状的思考 (Thoughts on the Development of "Gender Archaeology" in China). 文物鉴定与鉴赏 (*Identification and Appreciation of Cultural Relics*), (01), 174–177.

Yang Yueguang 杨月光 and Ai Wanqiao 艾婉乔 (2022). 柳湾马厂类型墓葬的定量考古学分析 (Quantitative Archaeological Analysis of Liuwan Machang-Type Tombs). 考古与文物 (*Archaeology and Cultural Relics*), (03), 121–128.

Yates, R. D. S. and Cai, D. (2018). Bibliography of Studies on Women and Gender in China since 2008. *Nan Nü*, 20(1), 3–152. https://doi.org/10.1163/15685268-00201P02 (accessed October 2, 2023).

Yong, Y. (2004). Gender, Status, Ritual Regulations, and Mortuary Practice in the State of Jin. In K. Linduff and Y. Sun, eds., *Gender and Chinese Archaeology*. Walnut Creek, CA: AltaMira, pp. 161–202.

Yong Ying 雍颖 (2006). 晋侯墓地性别、 地位、 礼制和葬仪分析 (Gender, Status, Ritual Regulations, and Mortuary Practice in the State of Jin). In Lin Jialin 林嘉琳 (Linduff, K. M.) and Sun Yan 孙岩 eds., 性别研究与中国考古学 (*Gender and Chinese Archaeology*), 北京大学震旦古代文明研究中心 (Aurora Center for the Study of Ancient Civilizations), 北京大学 (Beijing University). Beijing: Science Press, pp. 143–177.

Yoshie Akiko 義江明子 (1996). 日本古代の祭祀と女性 (Ancient Rituals and Women in Japan). 東京: Tōkyō: 吉川弘文館 Yoshikawa Kōbunkan.

(2000). 日本古代系譜様式論 (Theory of Ancient Japanese Genealogy Style). 東京: Tōkyō: 吉川弘文館 Yoshikawa Kōbunkan.

Yu Huanjin 于焕金 (2019). 性别视角下的东周墓葬研究 (Research on Eastern Zhou Tombs from the Perspective of Gender). Unpublished dissertation, Mentor: Teng Mingyu 滕铭予, Jilin University.

Zhang, B (2019). On the Change of the Female Status in the Tang Dynasty from the Horse-Riding Tomb Figurine. *Proceedings of the 2018 International Workshop on Education Reform and Social Sciences (ERSS 2018)*. Advances in Social Science, Education and Humanities Research (ASSEHR) (300). Amsterdam: Atlantis Press, pp. 589–594.

Zhang Chaohua 张超华 (2020). 性别考古视角中的王因墓地分析 (Analysis of Wang Yin's Graveyard from the Perspective of Gender Archaeology). 四川文物 (*Sichuan Cultural Relics*), (01), 107–116.

Zhang Liyan 张礼艳 (2016). 西周贵族墓葬所见性别差异 –– 兼论西周贵族妇女的社会地位 (Gender Differences in Western Zhou Noble Tombs: Also on the Social Status of Western Zhou Noble Women). 江汉考古 (*Jianghan Archaeology*), (04), 53–63.

Zhang Meifang 章梅芳 (2008). 中国性别考古学的开篇之作 – – 评《性别研究与中国考古学 (The Beginning of Chinese Gender Archaeology: Comment on Gender Studies and Chinese Archaeology). 中国科技史杂志 (*Chinese Journal of History of Science and Technology*), (01), 90–95.

Zhang Quanchao 张全超 (2005). 内蒙古和林格尔县新店子墓地人骨研究 (Research on Human Bones in Xindianzi Cemetery in Helinger County, Inner Mongolia). Unpublished dissertation, Mentor: Zhu Hong 朱泓, Jilin University.

Zhang Quanchao 张全超, Sun Yize 孙语泽, Hou Liangliang 侯亮亮, Ji Ping 吉平, and Zhu Yonggang 朱永刚 (2022). C、N稳定同位素分析 (C and N Stable Isotope Analysis of Human and Animal Skeletons at the Hamin Mangha Site). *Acta Anthropology*, 41(02), 261–273.

Zhang Qun 张群 (2018). 宁夏中卫常乐墓地人骨研究 (Research on Human Bones in Changle Cemetery of Zhongwei, Ningxia). Unpublished dissertation, Mentor: Zhang Quanchao 张全超, Jilin University.

Zhang Sen 张森 (2018). 东周时期齐国墓葬的性别考古分析 (Gender Archaeological Analysis of Qi State Tombs in the Eastern Zhou Dynasty). Unpublished dissertation, Mentors: Wang Qing 王青 and Liu Yanchang 刘延常, Shandong University.

Zhang Xu 张旭 (2015). 内蒙古和林格尔县大堡山墓地人骨研究 (Research on Human Bones in the Dabaoshan Cemetery in Helinger County, Inner Mongolia). Unpublished dissertation, Mentor: Zhu Hong 朱泓, Jilin University.

Zhang Xuelian 张雪莲 and Li Xinwei 李新伟 (2014). 西坡墓地再讨论 (Rediscussion on Xipo Cemetery). 中原文物 (*Central Plains Artifacts*), (04), 18–32.

Zhao Yongsheng 赵永生 (2013). 甘肃临潭磨沟墓地人骨研究 (Research on Human Bones in Mogou Cemetery in Lintan, Gansu). Unpublished dissertation, Mentor: Zhu Hong 朱泓, Jilin University.

Zheng Lanshuang 郑兰爽 (2012). 韩城梁带村芮国墓地出土人骨研究 (Research on Human Bones Unearthed from Ruiguo Cemetery in Liangdai Village, Hancheng). Unpublished dissertation, Mentor: Chen Liang 陈, Northwestern University.

Zhou Mi 周蜜 and Li Yongning 李永宁 (2010). 韩城梁带村芮国墓地出土人骨研究 (A Preliminary Study on Human Bones Unearthed from Longkou Tombs in Danjiang Reservoir Area). 江汉考古 (*Jianghan Archaeology*), (01), 108–112.

Zhou Yawei 周亚威 (2014). 北京延庆西屯墓地人骨研究 (Research on Human Bones in Xitun Cemetery, Yanqing, Beijing). Unpublished dissertation, Mentor: Zhu Hong 朱泓, Jilin University.

Acknowledgements

We would like to recognize the assistance of the following people whose help was essential in both finding and reviewing secondary literature:

China: Tzehuey Chiou-Peng – for reading and critiquing the section on China and for contact information on Zhang Mei and her article on female archaeologists in China.

Japan: Junko Habu – for references to Japanese archaeologists working on gender; Fumiko Ikawa-Smith – for her syllabus on gendered archaeology; Karen Gerhart – for advice on the Japan section of the Element; Asumi Oba for assistance with Japanese articles.

Korea: Jae-Hoon Shim (Dankook University, Department of History, Yong'in); Jungeun Lee – for advice on the Korea essay and contacting Shim.

Mongolia: Jean-Luc Houle – for information on gender studies in Mongolia.

Taiwan: Ting-yu Yen – for information about gender studies in Taiwan.

We would like to thank the Faculty Research Grant program of Hanover College for financial support.

Two anonymous reviewers of the Element provided suggestions that strengthened our arguments and clarified what we found. Their contributions are much appreciated. Finally, thanks must also go to Rowan Flad, coeditor of this series, who called out our mistakes, questioned our often too streamlined prose, and gently challenged our thinking. His and the other critiques pushed us to elaborate and strengthen our own understanding of the issues.

Cambridge Elements

Ancient East Asia

About the Series

Elements in Ancient East Asia contains multi-disciplinary contributions focusing on the history and culture of East Asia in ancient times. Its framework extends beyond anachronistic, nation-based conceptions of the past, following instead the contours of Asian sub-regions and their interconnections with each other. Within the series there are five thematic groups: 'Sources', which includes excavated texts and other new sources of data; 'Environments', exploring interaction zones of ancient East Asia and long-distance connections; 'Institutions', including the state and its military; 'People', including family, gender, class, and the individual and 'Ideas', concerning religion and philosophy, as well as the arts and sciences. The series presents the latest findings and strikingly new perspectives on the ancient world in East Asia.

Cambridge Elements

Ancient East Asia

Elements in the Series

Violence and the Rise of Centralized States in East Asia
Mark Edward Lewis

Bronze Age Maritime and Warrior Dynamics in Island East Asia
Mark Hudson

Medicine and Healing in Ancient East Asia: A View from Excavated Texts
Constance A. Cook

The Methods and Ethics of Researching Unprovenienced Artifacts from East Asia
Christopher J. Foster, Glenda Chao and Mercedes Valmisa

Environmental Foundations to the Rise of Early Civilisations in China
Yijie Zhuang

Archaeological Studies on Gender in Early East Asia
Mandy Jui-man Wu and Katheryn M. Linduff

A full series listing is available at: www.cambridge.org/EAEA

For EU product safety concerns, contact us at Calle de José Abascal, 56–1°, 28003 Madrid, Spain or eugpsr@cambridge.org.

www.ingramcontent.com/pod-product-compliance
Ingram Content Group UK Ltd.
Pitfield, Milton Keynes, MK11 3LW, UK
UKHW022145080726
473066UK00010B/776

* 9 7 8 1 1 0 8 9 8 7 3 9 4 *